Tar Heel
Tombstones
and the Tales They Tell

Tar Heel Tombstones
and the Tales They Tell

Henry King

Down Home Press, P.O. Box 4126, Asheboro, N.C. 27204

First Printing, April, 1990
Second Printing, November, 1990
Third Printing, Revised, April, 1993

ISBN 0-9624255-2-4

Library of Congress Catalog Card Number 90-060344

Printed in the United States of America

Cover design by Harry Blair
Book design by Elizabeth House

Down Home Press
P.O. Box 4126
Asheboro, N.C. 27204

For
My Son
Maxton
Who Had More Than Average Familiarity
With Graveyards During Boyhood.
On Sandy Creek He Found The Grave
Of William Trogdon Whose Epitaph
Told A Tale Of Derring-Do And Murder
During The Revolutionary War.

His Bedroom Window Faced The Baptist Cemetery
Across The Street And He Often Took
Short Cuts Through That Graveyard To Reach
His Grandmother Frazier's Country Store.

And In That Same Graveyard He Came Close To
Having A Fatal Accident.
He Overlooked The Danger Of Trying To Sled
Down An Icy Slope Dotted With Tombstones.
His Head Missed The Monument He Struck
But His Leg Was Severely Injured.
He Carries The Scars To This Day.

In That Cemetery Is An Epitaph He Well Remembers:
"Sick And Sore She Longtime Bore,
Physicians Were In Vain..."

Acknowledgments

Most of the material in this book is new, but small portions originally appeared in slightly different form in *The Courier-Tribune* of Asheboro and are used with permission.

Generally, those who gave their time and shared information are named in the text, but others were also helpful, including: Crisp Dixon, Siler City; Rev. Waldo Dodson, Sanford; Louise Wilson, Snow Camp Drama Society; Brenda Marshburn, Brunswick Town; Eugenia Lore, Concord; John R. Woodard, archivist, Wake Forest University; Barbara O'Neil, Beaufort Historical Society; Jane H. McCann, Harnett County Library; The Rev. Marion Terry, Fuquay-Varina; Dennis Rogers, the Raleigh *News & Observer;* Carol and Eddie Stevenson, Liberty; and Louise Dawkins, Rockingham Municipal Library.

All photographs were taken by the author except for that of the "Slave Joe" tombstone, which was made by Edward Stevenson of Liberty. Thanks is due Ron Baker of Happy Hollow for aid and advice with photo reproduction.

And I owe a large measure of appreciation to my wife Maxine for invaluable aid during many hours in the field where she helped decipher and copy indistinct epitaphs amid briers and bumblebees.

Foreword

You may safely laugh in the face of anyone who tells you this epitaph is to be found "somewhere in North Carolina."

> *Ma loved Pa.*
> *Pa loved wimmen.*
> *Ma found Pa*
> *With one in swimmin.*
> *Here lies Pa.*

Likewise, scoff if someone tells with a straight face that "somewhere" a Tar Heel cemetery has an epitaph with these words:

> *Here lies John O'Day.*
> *He lived the life of Riley.*
> *While Riley was away.*

Those are among the epitaphs repeated often whenever tall tales about graveyards are told. No such epitaphs exist, although they have been reported for nearly a century.

Even so, you can enter a cemetery heavy-hearted and walk out with a smile. Mrs. Alice R. Roper of Pittsboro would have wanted that. Her epitaph at the county seat of Chatham County says:

> *She Left A Legacy Of Laughter.*

An old adage declares that we are "born to die." But the

epitaph of G. F. Morris at the city cemetery at Troy in Montgomery County insists:

Death is but another life.

So maybe the end is not the end at all, even though a cemetery is our last address. There, in the "Marble Orchard of Memories," you'll sometimes find surprises.

A graveyard can be an outdoor classroom. Among its lessons are history and philosophy. Humor abounds too.

Contents

The grave of the Rev. J.T. Arrington, in the Old Burying Grounds in Beaufort in Carteret County.

Greeting the Grim Reaper

When Vermont's Revolutionary War hero Ethan Allen lay on his deathbed breathing his last, his preacher sought to reassure him.

"Fear not, Mr. Allen," he said. "The angels are waiting at the Pearly Gates."

"Well dammit," replied the crusty Allen, raising himself on one elbow, "let them wait!"

But when death knocked on the door of North Carolina's youthful J.T. Arrington, he was not like Ethan Allen. Arrington seemed joyous about making the journey, if we are to believe his epitaph:

In death he sang
The Old Ship Of Zion
And with triumphal song
Crossed the river
To join the singers
On the other side.

Humble in life — triumphant in death
— in Heaven at home.

Arrington's grave is in the Old Burying Ground at Beaufort in Carteret County. The grave of Ethan Allen (1737-89) is at Greenmount Cemetery in Burlington, Vt. It is marked by a 42-foot granite shaft topped with a statue of Allen with arms upraised.

Posthumorously Speaking

Why it was listed as an obituary rather than an epitaph is not known, but the late Carl Goerch once carried this item in his newspaper column:

OBITUARY
In
The Raleigh (N.C.) Star
March 1, 1810

"Beneath This Stone,
A Lump Of Clay.
Lies Arabella Young;
Who On The 24th Day Of May
Began To Hold her Tongue."

This epitaph also has been reported as being in Hatfield, Mass., and even England, so it may be apocryphal. But North Carolina has an epitaph that, if misinterpreted, could be compared to Arabella Young's for the impression it inadvertently gives.

The stone on Martha Clark's grave at Cedar Grove Cemetery in New Bern states:

Wife Of William Clark
D. 1839 Age 83.

She Was A Member of
The Baptist Church

There Remaineth Therefore
A Rest To The People Of God.

* * *

PRAISES ON TOMBSTONES
ARE BUT IDLY SPENT;
A MAN'S GOOD NAME
IS HIS BEST MONUMENT.

So says the tombstone of Samuel Leffers at Beaufort in Carteret County. Leffers wrote the words himself, revealing them first in a letter to his brother John in New York on April 9, 1806.

"I wrote my own epitaph some years ago," he said, "and although it may never be engraved on stone, you may read it for your own amusement:

'Praises on Tombs are vainly spent;
Good deeds are a man's best monument.'

"Having thus hinted at what ought to be man's principal concern, I now descend to the common affairs of the world..."

It would be 16 more years before Leffers died, and by then he had slightly revised his epitaph. His brother John saw that the words were engraved on his tombstone.

Leffers' tomb is in The Old Burying Ground along Ann Street in Beaufort. Leffers and his wife Sarah owned what is known today as the Leffers' House on the Beaufort Historical Association grounds. They also lived in the Hammock, which is Beaufort's oldest dwelling.

* * *

Whether Thomas Lassiter gave people short answers is not known. Likely, he was a man of few words, especially if someone asked him something personal. All that is assumption, but it is backed up by some strong words on his tombstone:

He Was Noted For
Attending To His Own Business
And Letting Others' Business
Alone.

Lassiter, a strongly religious man, was 57 in 1860, when he was laid to rest at Oak Grove Cemetery near Lassiter's Mill along

Tom Lassiter is buried at Oak Grove Cemetery near Lassiter's Mill along Secondary Road 1175 in Randolph County.

Secondary Road 1175 in southern Randolph County. Part of the inscription on his tombstone states:

> *He was for 32 years an acceptable*
> *member of the M.E. Church, a liberal*
> *supporter of the gospel and every*
> *good cause and believed in Christ-*
> *ianity and served God from principle*
> *rather than from vain show.*

Mrs. Ruby Lassiter Culver of Randleman, a family historian, says the Lassiter name comes from the English "Leicester." The name, she said, means "walled town or camp on the River Legrs."

In a sense, Tom Lassiter's character was a personification of that. He thought that every person was entitled to keep his affairs behind the invisible wall of privacy, and he had that belief spelled out on his tombstone.

> *Truth And Honesty Characterized*
> *All His Dealings*
> *With Men*
> *And He Was Noted For*
> *Attending To His Own Business*
> *And Letting Others' Business Alone.*

* * *

Tom Lassiter would have been the perfect neighbor for Mrs. Mary Lefavour. She died in 1797 and was buried in Pine Grove Cemetery on U.S. Highway 77 at Topsfield, Mass.

Her tombstone says:

> *Reader pass on, ne'er waste your time*
> *On bad biography or bitter rhyme.*
> *For what I am, this umb'rous clay ensures,*
> *And what I was, is no affair of yours.*

The Final Curtain

Professor Antoine Danton jumped to a conclusion. His epitaph says so.

LEAPED FROM LIFE INTO ETERNITY.

He did that. Literally.

Danton was a performer with a traveling tent show whose specialty was diving from a tall tower into a tiny tank of water.

He jumped from way up there...

...To

      way

          down

              here...

...And missed his mark.

He started 100 feet in the air. He ended six feet underground in Maplewood Cemetery in Wilson. Danton was billed by the J.J. Jones Carnival Company as a "dashing, fearless, intrepid high diver" when the show came to town in May, 1904. A native of Hungary, he assumed the title of professor. He had dark, good looks and an intriguing accent. A man of muscles. Women swooned when he appeared in diving tights.

Crowds flocked to see the "unbelievable, death-defying" Danton dive from 90 feet into a small tank of water that had a burning liquid on its surface.

Danton made many friends in Wilson, including one young woman with whom he became particularly enamored, and when the carnival moved on to its next stop at nearby Goldsboro, an entourage of admirers followed, bringing him gifts, including champagne.

Danton's tent was a happy place on the afternoon and early evening of May 13. Friends and strangers crowded around, urging toasts to the famed, dashing figure. No one knows how many toasts Danton may have shared or how potent any of the liquids may have been. Rumors later had it that when the time for his performance arrived after sundown the professor did not seem steady on his feet. But his words were as bold as ever. He'd climb to the very top of the 100 foot tower, he declared, and beat his own high dive mark by 10 feet.

The crowd watched in awe as he ascended.

Oldtimers say the usual procedure called for a helper to set fire to oil floating on the water in the tank into which Danton would dive. Danton would then set fire to part of his oiled costume and leap for the mark, making a spectacular fireworks descent into the small, flaming circle below.

Danton saw the flames appear on the tank beneath him. He put a match to his costume. But in that second, the fire below flickered low. Some say it went out entirely. Already aflame himself, Danton had no choice but to jump for a target he couldn't see well. Instead of his usual splash at the end of a dramatic drum roll, he made only a sickening thud, accompanied by screams from the crowd.

As he lay dying from his injuries, Danton reportedly whispered that he wanted to be taken back to Wilson to be buried because he had made so many friends in that town and the love of his life lived there.

The carnival band played a mournful, graveside tune when his request was carried out.

Performers of the Jones Show raised money not only for the funeral but for an unusual grave marker as well. It states:

Prof. A. Danton, the intrepid high diver, leaped from life into eternity at Goldsboro, May 13, 1904. Erected by the J. J. Jones Carnival Company of which organization the deceased was, at the time of making the fatal leap, a member.

The grave is just inside the entrance of Maplewood Cemetery.

* * *

A marker considered unique in graveyard architecture adorns the grave of John King in Charlotte's Elmwood Cemetery on West 6th Street. Shaped like a miniature Washington Monument, the stained marble marker bears the figure of an elephant carved by Billy Berryhill, a Confederate veteran who became renown for his tombstone carvings.

A brief inscription on the stone explains the intriguing presence of the pachyderm but offers few details.

In Memory Of John King
Killed At Charlotte, N.C.
Sept. 27, 1880
By Elephant Chief
May His Soul Rest In Peace.

On that bright autumn day when John King died, there was excitement in Mecklenburg County. The circus was coming. It had played the previous night in nearby Concord, and advance word was that it was a humdinger of a show.

By late afternoon the first units were arriving on railway cars. The horse-drawn circus wagons would be straggling in after dusk. Two shows would be held the next day. The dirt roads leading to the show grounds were heavy with wagon traffic as farmers and their families came to watch the circus set up. For many local people, the prelude to the circus was almost as much fun as the performance itself.

Family groups were thick about the grounds when a terrifying scream arose. An elephant was loose and running amuck! The crowds seemed stunned at first, then broke to run. A few spectators saw a huge elephant named Chief charge into his keeper, John King, who fell and was trampled, screaming in agony.

Circus workers grabbed tent poles to go after the elephant, while others dashed into nearby stores to grab hoes and rakes to use as prods and weapons.

After a short flight, Chief was corralled near Fifth Street by several men brandishing pitchforks and other tools. The angry beast was calmed enough to be chained to another elephant that was brought to the scene. Chief returned to the fairgrounds a prisoner.

John King, a worker with the circus, was killed by an elephant when the circus passed through Mecklenburg County in 1880.

According to some accounts, John King died shortly after being carried to a barber shop on nearby Trade Street, where towels and alcohol were available for first aid. A Dr. McCombs reportedly was summoned and declared King beyond medical help.

The next morning, the body was taken to Elmwood Cemetery where King was given final rites by a priest. The circus band played an out-of-tune funeral march because the musicians knew only snappy circus tunes.

According to one account of the burial, written by Majel Ivey Seay in *The State* magazine in 1961, two circus elephants, Boy and Mary, were also brought to the gravesite. Chief was kept elsewhere, in chains.

On its annual tour in Charlotte each year afterwards, members of the circus took elephants and the band to the graveyard for a brief memorial service.

Chief was never allowed to perform in any circus act after King was killed, but he was allowed in street parades where keepers could manage him because he wore heavy leg chains. After the circus folded, it was reported that Chief was given to a Cincinnati zoo and was sentenced to die after killing two more keepers. Poisoned food was tried but failed to kill him. So he was hanged by the neck with a noose made of steel cable and hoisted by a derrick.

* * *

When Italian carnival worker "Forenzio W. Concippio" was hit on the head with an iron-rimmed wooden tent stake and killed during an argument in 1911, no one seemed to be able to pronounce his odd, foreign-sounding name. So people around Laurinburg in Scotland County just called the dead man "Spaghetti."

What is stranger than his name is that he died when he was 23 years old, but he wasn't buried until he was 84. And all that time he was on view at the funeral home.

The story began at the tiny town of McColl, S.C., eight miles south of Laurinburg. The man who brought the dead carnival worker to McDougald Funeral Home on U.S. Highway 74-B in Laurinburg said the corpse was his son. The late John McDougald did not speak Italian, and the man spoke only a few words of heavily-accented

English. McDougald was never able to fully understand the man or correctly spell the name of the deceased, but he did the best he could, writing down what he understood was "Forenzio Concippio."

The man left a small down payment for funeral, indicating he would be back with the rest. The body was embalmed and placed in a coffin. The funeral home waited for burial instructions. Days, weeks, months, and years went by. The father never returned. Eventually the body and the tent "stob" evidence were transferred to a glass-topped box and stowed in a rear room. Finally, both were put in the garage, where the box stood upright.

Through the years, as the body mummified, more and more visitors asked to see it. For decades Spaghetti was a local curiosity, but he attracted tourists too.

In 1970, the story of Spaghetti was told in a book, *Carnival*, by Arthur H. Lewis, Trident Press. A spate of other stories followed, and in early September, 1972, *The Laurinburg Exchange* reported rumors that the burial of Spaghetti might be imminent. One rumor indicated an offer had been made to bury Spaghetti at "Carneytown" in Florida. Another was that the Italian Embassy had been approached to do something and that the Roman Catholic Church would make an attempt to get the body buried.

The story of Spaghetti became so popular that even the national newspaper *Grit* carried an article about it. With Spaghetti becoming an issue, the funeral home stopped viewing of his body.

A congressman of Italian ancestry, Representative Mario Biaggi of New York, vociferously protested the long-delayed funeral but sought without success to get help for burial from North Carolina's congressional delegation. He also wrote to state legislators to no avail.

Funeral home officials said they were abiding by an oral agreement of many years, awaiting instructions from kinfolk and arrangements for payment. There was wild talk that a "storage fee" for the body was $22,000. But the fee was actually only 25 cents per day, for a total of $5,000, most of which the funeral home expected to waive.

Rumors that Congressman Biaggi was heading up a fund drive to cover funeral costs did not turn out to be true.

"When I was contacted by that person, it was by letter that

included a five dollar check," Hewitt McDougald said. "It had been mailed in a government-franked envelope. I sent it back, putting a stamp on an envelope marked, 'Paid for by McDougald Funeral Home.' "

Actually, McDougald felt the main issue was that if Spaghetti was to be buried without instructions from family members, it would be done by the funeral home, and the funeral would be at Laurinburg, because Spaghetti had become a town legend and townspeople felt he should be buried there. With those thoughts in mind, and to avoid any further controversy, McDougald decided to bury Spaghetti.

"When the time came, Spaghetti's funeral was paid for by someone right here in town," McDougald said. "I was asked not to tell who paid for it. I have never told, and I never will as long as I live."

According to a story in *The Laurinburg Exchange* on September 30, 1972, Spaghetti was buried at Hillside Cemetery in a bronze casket and a porcelain vault, the best available.

"McDougald himself provided the casket wreath, a marker and a shroud," the story said. "As an extra precaution some concrete was poured atop the vault to make it inaccessible. There was no obituary."

A marble marker was put at the gravesite of "Forenzio Concippio" at Hillside Cemetery off U.S. Highway 401. But Spaghetti's story was not finished. McDougald said he wanted to make certain the handwritten records on file at the funeral home were compatible with those on the courthouse death certificate.

"I sent my son Beachum up there and he came back with the surprising information that records showed that Spaghetti's name was not Forenzio Concippio, as my father had written it down many years ago. Beachum found the actual name of the victim was Cancetto Farmica."

So, a handsome bronze plaque with the correct name, date, and age was fashioned to replace the marble marker.

Cancetto Farmica
Age 23
Died April 28, 1911
Buried Sep. 30, 1972.

"We still get phone calls and letters about Spaghetti," said Hewitt McDougald. "People from other parts of the country still stop by and ask to see him, not knowing we buried him in 1972."

* * *

The grave of Siamese twins Eng and Chang Bunker

As twins to mortal life we came
As twins we rest together.
As twins we hope to rise again
As twins with Christ forever.
--Epitaph on a double headstone in Wilmington

Two sets of the world's most renowned twins lived and died in

North Carolina, and the eye-catching epitaphs on their tombstones still cause passersby to stop and reflect about their curious lives.

At White Plains in Surry County, the epitaph of Eng and Chang Bunker is one known around the globe:

Siamese Twins.

* * *

On their modest marker near Whiteville, in Columbus County, Mille-Christine McCoy appropriately share a couplet:

A soul with two thoughts;
Two hearts that beat as one.

Physically bound together at birth and at the time surgically inseparable, both sets of twins found international fame and fortune in show business. The Bunker brothers died in 1874, the McCoy sisters in 1912.

Known the world over as "The Siamese Twins," Chang and Eng Bunker were joined at midriff by a heavy band of flesh. They were born in Siam (now Thailand) in 1811. Their parents, however, were Chinese. Their father died when they were about eight. When the twins were in their late teens, their mother, who had nine children to look after, permitted an American ship captain to take her twin sons abroad for exhibition.

When they became 21, the twins took control of their own lives and traveled the world in show business. They saved their money and planned someday to give up the circuit for a home and family. Two North Carolina girls hastened that day. Sisters, they fell in love with Eng and Chang and agreed to marriage.

The twins met Sarah and Adelaide Yates in 1839 when they came to Wilkes County to put on a show and to hunt and fish at the invitation of a local doctor. They stayed three weeks, taking part in local social functions, even dancing with the Yates sisters.

During the next four years the Siamese Twins visited Wilkes County often, calling on Sarah and Adelaide. In 1843 they married, Chang to Adelaide, Eng to Sarah. They bought a farm at Trap Hill, but 10 years later moved to Surry County, where each couple built a house and started a family. Ten children eventually were born to Chang and Adelaide, 11 to Eng and Sarah. Although the families lived separately, the twins alternated spending three days at each household.

Chang developed poor health at age 58 after suffering a stroke in 1869. He died on January 17, 1874. Eng awoke from a sound sleep to find his brother dead. Two hours later, he too was dead. Their grave is in White Plains Church Cemetery, 100 yards west of old U.S. Highway 601, four miles south of Mt. Airy.

Mille-Christine, who were called the Carolina Twins, used a hyphenated name because they considered themselves one. Born into slavery in 1851 on the plantation of Jabez McCoy at Welches Creek in Columbus County, the twins were perfectly formed but joined at the lower spine, making it difficult for each to turn and see the other's face.

Their owner sold them as curiosities when they were a year old, and they were sold a second time when they were four and already being exhibited overseas. The twins learned to sing and give recitations, appearing even before crowned heads of Europe. By the time the Civil War broke out, they were back in America under ownership of Joe P. Smith of Wadesboro, who hid them in South Carolina to keep them from federal troops.

Freed after the war, Mille-Christine promptly hired a manager, perfected their skills and went on tour again. They mastered seven languages and accrued a fortune of some $500,000 before they retired in 1892. Ironically, they bought part of the old plantation on which they were born and built a huge house for themselves. When the house was destroyed by fire in 1909, they built a smaller home so that they could give more money to schools and churches rather than spending it on themselves.

A few years later, Mille developed tuberculosis, and the twins spent several months in a sanatorium, but Mille's condition worsened, and she died on October 8, 1912 at 61. Attached to her dead sister's body, Christine lay abed singing hymns and praying until she died about 12 hours later.

Mille-Christine were buried near their home, but in the late

27

1960s, after the site was damaged by fire, the local historical society obtained permission to move the double grave to Welches Creek Cemetery along Secondary Road 1719. A new granite marker was erected to take the place of the old fire-scorched metal one.

Engraved on Mille's side of the stone is this:

Born July 11, 1851, Columbus County. A child of Jacob and Monemia McCoy. She lived a life of much comfort owing to her love of God and joy in following His commands. A real friend to the needy of both races and loved by all who knew her.

The engraving on Christine's side reads:

Died Oct. 8th and 9th 1912, fully resigned at home, the place of her birth and residence of her parents.

"They that be planted in the house of the Lord shall flourish in the courts of our God. Psalms 92;13."

Psalms 139, verses 13 and 14 were the favorite Biblical selections of Mille-Christine:

"For thou has possessed my reins: thou hast covered me in my mother's womb. I will praise thee; for I am fearfully and wonderfully made: marvelous are Thy works; and that my soul knoweth right well."

* * *

He was a trick rider in the circus, but the marble slab over his grave in Cabarrus County uses a misspelled fancy word to explain his occupation.

In Memory Of
George Yeomin
"Equestrin."

Little is known of George Yeomin other than that he was born in Edinburg, Scotland, on January 13, 1801. He reportedly died from injuries received in a fall from his horse on November 7, 1827, at Salisbury, shortly before a scheduled performance.

Noboby knows just how Yeomin died, but the generally accepted explanation is that he was riding his favorite mount during a street parade and fell for some unknown reason.

There was an elephant in the parade just behind him, and he may have been stepped on by the huge animal. Critically injured, he was carried 20 miles to Concord for medical treatment, but there was no hospital in the town. To the further dismay of those who assisted him, the local inn was full, and he could not be temporarily cared for there. Instead, he was taken to a private home, the Fourd House, where he succumbed to his injuries.

Yeomin's ivy-entwined tomb is at First Presbyterian Church Memorial Garden on Spring Street in downtown Concord, a beautifully landscaped old burial ground on the site where the church was first constructed in 1804. It can be found by taking a left inside the entrance and following the pathway. Many names and initials are crudely scratched into the marble slab atop the tomb, thought to have been put there by circus performers whose shows played nearby and visited out of respect to a fallen comrade.

Among the names is that of J. Riley, dated 1880, followed by the word "juggler," indicating that performers continued to visit the grave for decades after Yeomin's death.

They Milked Life
and Shared the Cream

Ashes to ashes and dust to dust;
If the Lord doesn't get you
The devil must.
— Old Folk Saying

From the graveyards of the mountains to cemeteries of the seashore, epitaphs across North Carolina remind passersby to make a choice while they may.

James Patterson, who died at 18 in 1829, has these graphic words on his tombstone at the Olney Presbyterian Church Cemetery at Gastonia in Gaston County:

When this you see, remember me,
Lest I be forgotten:
When I am dead and in the grave
And all my bones are rotten.

* * *

D.S. Lentz was not so morbid about his state. Buried at Organ Lutheran Church along Secondary Road 1006 in Rowan County, he was philosophical when he died in 1915 at age 47:

Sometime I'll wake,
I know not where.
I only know God will be there.
Relieved of all that hindrance here,
I'll fill a broader, nobler sphere.
So do not weep, but wear a smile.
I've just lay down to rest a while.

* * *

Mary Bethune lived to be 90 and was buried in 1846 at Bethesda Cemetery along N.C. Highway 5 east of Aberdeen in Moore County. She left behind this message:

Adieu kind friends
This stone will show
That my remains are placed below.
My stay was long with you below
But long or short we all must go.
Therefore prepare to meet your God
Before you're laid beneath the sod:
There are no acts of pardon found
In the cold grave to which you're bound.

* * *

Parting was not sweet sorrow to 78-year-old George Ratcliff Pilkenton who died in 1944. His epitaph in St. Bartholomew Episcopal Church Cemetery at Pittsboro in Chatham County assures the world:

To him death is no conqueror.
At the end he simply smiled
To greet another friend.

* * *

31

At St. Peter's Episcopal Church Cemetery at Washington in Beaufort County, as well as at dozens of other graveyards across the state, is an epitaph often seen. It has variations, but this is the dire warning on James Foreman's headstone:

Come view my tomb, as you pass by;
As you are now, so once was I.
As I am now, soon you must be,
Therefore prepare to follow me.

* * *

Many are the graveyard browsers who have noticed that vandals sometimes deface that epitaph by adding postcripts such as these:

To follow you I'm not content,
Until I know which way you went.

Your comment leaves me with a frown.
Did you go up, or did you go down?

* * *

"Miss Jo" Williams always looked upon young men with a soft heart. On her tombstone in Gum Orchard Baptist Church Cemetery at Zephyr in Surry County are these words:

She Gave Her Love And Support
To The Boys
At Old Wake Forest
For Over Forty Years.

Joanna Williams, always called Miss Jo, was single and 36 when she went to the community of Wake Forest in Wake County in 1924. She was what folks in those days called an "old maid." And there may have been some eyebrows raised when she opened a boarding house for male college students.

Characterized as tiny and durable, Miss Jo became known over the years to thousands of students on the campus of Wake Forest College.

Some years after opening the boarding house, she also opened a cafeteria which became the favorite eating place for students and faculty alike. She continued the service until 1956 when the college was moved to Winston-Salem in Forsyth County.

She was 68 at the time, well into retirement age, so during the next four years she slowly phased out her business. Then she followed her beloved Wake Forest boys and built a home on Reynolda Road in Winston-Salem.

When Joanna Williams died in July, 1974, at 85, an obituary in the *Winston-Salem Journal* stated: "A large number of students helped pay their way through college working for Miss Williams, who probably had little use for the women's liberation movement. She said she was not particularly pleased when Wake Forest became coeducational in the mid-1940s.

"On Sundays her preference was noticeable when she would walk through the cafeteria giving extra pieces of chicken to the customers. The best and biggest pieces went to the men."

She liked the fellows to call her "Miss Jo," and that is what is on her tombstone.

* * *

Like Miss Jo, many others across North Carolina have given their time, talents, and even their lives to others, and their tombstones make it known.

Sarah Vaughn Caviness died in 1908 at 25. She was buried at Concord Cemetery at the junction of Secondary Roads 2636 and 2640, a half mile northeast of Coleridge in Randolph County.

Her mission in life
Was to give others pleasure.

* * *

Five words sum up the life of Pearl Johnson Huffman, who died in 1979 at 86. She was buried at Springfield Baptist Church Cemetery east of Whitsett in Guilford County:

Never Too Busy To Care.

* * *

At right, the Aberdeen grave of Colin Bethune, 'an honest man.' Below, Joanna Williams, a faithful supporter of 'Old Wake Forest.'

Dell Headen, at front in the photo at left, was buried with his Scout uniform on. His grave, shown below, has a symbol of Scouting as well as the Scout motto, 'Be Prepared.'

DELL THOMAS, SON OF
J. & MINNIE HEADEN
MAR. 6, 1931
MAY 21, 1945

John D. Hughes did not have to die in 1879 at age 24, but he put his life on the line that others might live. Hughes is buried in Cedar Grove Cemetery at New Bern in Craven County:

Drowned Aug. 18. 1879
During the great storm
At Beaufort, N.C.,
Striving to save the lives
Of others.

"Greater love hath no man than this.
That a man lay down his life
For his friends."

* * *

Camille L. Jerome is buried at Pittsboro, the county seat of Chatham County. Her epitaph at St. Bartholomew Church Cemetery says:

All who knew her
And many who knew her not,
Are better that she has lived.

* * *

Ida C. Justice devoted herself to looking after her family, and upon her death in 1942 at 63, her tombstone in Sapling Ridge Cemetery in Chatham County was marked with these words:

She Made Home Pleasant.

* * *

The life of Lucy McLean, who is buried in The Old Burying Ground at Beaufort, was marked, as is her grave, by simplicity:

She hath done what she could.

* * *

Diogenes, the Greek philosopher and cynic who went about with a lighted lantern looking for an honest man, might have found his quarry in North Carolina if epitaphs are to be believed.

A good example is James P. Dozier, 1834-1918, who is buried at Providence Friends Cemetery along Secondary Road 2113 northeast of Randleman in Randolph County.

A simple, honest, truthful man.

* * *

J. T. Johnson also would qualify. He is buried at Pleasant Hill Church Cemetery along Secondary Road 2371 in southwest Alamance County. Johnson's brief epitaph proclaims him:

A truthful man.

* * *

John M. Bateman, who died in 1914 at age 79 and is buried in Grace Episcopal Church Cemetery at Plymouth in Washington County, apparently was a better man than his time.

Upright and just in all his ways.
A bright example in degenerate days.

* * *

Colin Bethune, a physician, is buried east of Aberdeen in Moore County, at the Bethesda Presbyterian Church Cemetery along Secondary Road 2074. He requested these words be placed upon his tombstone:

A native of Scotland
By accident
But a citizen of the U.S.
From Choice

Somebody also added this afterthought to his name:

(An Honest Man)

* * *

A wit's a feather,
And a chief's a rod;
An honest man's
The noblest work of God.

Those words decorate the headstone of Malachi Haughton, a lawyer buried at St. Paul's Church at Edenton in Chowan County. Family members also added these words of praise.

Adored with the virtues of providence.
Temperance, integrity, and truth.
An affectionate husband, indulgent father.
Kind master, sincere friend.
Universally respected and esteemed.

* * *

The most prominent words on Dell Headen's tombstone are:

Be Prepared.

The Boy Scout motto is engraved as part of a compass symbol that encloses an American eagle. His grave is on the crest of a hill at Hope Methodist and Bonlee Baptist Church Cemetery, along Secondary Road 1005 in western Chatham County.

"He was my brother," said Margaret Headen Tillman at Tillman's Service Station along old U. S. Highway 421 in Bonlee, only a quarter of a mile from the cemetery. "Our family lived up at Siler City back then, back in 1945, when my brother died. I was only 15 myself, a year older than he.

"We called him 'Wart.' The family and friends called him that because he was somewhat small. Although not very tall, he was a happy, friendly boy and would do almost anything for you. His reddish hair and freckled face stood out in a crowd, and he was a popular boy.

"Somewhere along the way, when he was a small boy, too small to join the Boy Scouts, he'd hang around them anyway, always watching and interested in what they were doing. The first thing he did when he turned old enough was to become a Scout. He joined Troop 24 in Siler City. Oh, he loved Scouting. It was something he was always talking about or working on some project for his troop."

Dell earned many honors in Scouting and his family kept a record of them in a scrapbook. He was so well known and liked that when he fell seriously ill, the entire town became concerned.

"He had suffered a ruptured appendix," Mrs. Tillman said, "and he was hospitalized. For awhile, it looked as though he would recover, but peritonitis set in and he died."

During his illness, the young Scout became a rallying point for a town under strain of World War II. Letters, cards and telephone calls swamped the local hospital, not only from friends but from others who had never met him. Newspapers began to carry bulletins of his condition.

An old clipping states, "...local doctors and many members of the hospital staff interested themselves in the young man's case as though he were the only patient they had. The people in the community kept the telephones busy day and night, inquiring about his welfare..."

"That youngster's sickness and his untimely passing has done more to bring out the Christian spirit of our people than anything I have ever known," a local citizen wrote in a letter to the editor.

"My mother and father knew how much he loved Scouting...how much it meant to him," Mrs. Tillman said. "He loved it so much the family decided he should have a Scout symbol on his headstone...they had him buried in his Boy Scout uniform."

In his memory, the Dell Headen Scout Honor Award was established. It is still given every year.

His grave shows that Alton Stewart was the first licensed pilot in North Carolina.

Wings, Whistles, and Wheels

North Carolinians know from their car tags that their state is "First In Flight," but how many know who was the first Tar Heel to be given a license to fly?

That honor went to Alton Stewart of Dunn in Harnett County, and the signature on the license was a famous one: Orville Wright.

As fate would have it, Stewart would eventually die in an airplane crash. The tragedy is told on his tombstone in sad words:

Broken Wings, 1929.

A tombstone is depicted on the headstone at Stewart's grave at Coats Family Cemetery at Jackson and Patterson Streets in Coats, another Harnett County town, and it bears its own epitaph:

He
Died In Man's
Conquest
Of The
Air

Stewart was a pioneer aviator who started flying in the 1920s when airplanes were fragile and pilots "flew by the seat of their pants." Born in 1897, he was six years old when the Wright Brothers astounded the world by making the first powered flight at Kitty Hawk. By the time Stewart reached his teens, the U.S. Army was using biplanes and some were based at Polk Field, later to be known as Polk Air Force Base near Fayetteville.

One day in 1919, an army plane flew over the auto repair shop where Stewart worked. Its engine was cutting off, and the pilot made an emergency landing in a nearby cotton field. Stewart hurried over to the plane to ask if he could help, and the pilot let him check the engine. Repairs would take several days, Stewart discovered, but the pilot told him to go ahead and make them.

Within a week, Stewart had the engine purring again, and when the pilot took off, gained altitude, circled and waved, Stewart figured that both the airplane and aviation had left his life forever. But the pilot circled again and landed.

He had returned, he told a surprised Stewart, to give him a complimentary ride for his work. Stewart jumped at the chance. He was overjoyed when the pilot invited him to visit the military airfield, where Army pilots gave him flying lessons.

That prompted Stewart to buy an old biplane, becoming the first civilian in North Carolina to own an aircraft, although he did not yet have a pilot's permit. But in the spring of 1924, with a military co-pilot as witness, he took his first solo flight and sought his license, submitting his credentials to federal authorities. One of those officials was Orville Wright, who traveled to the "home field" of applying pilots to give them a check flight and to certify them personally.

Wright signed the original document that Stewart received in 1926, and the signature is reproduced on Stewart's tombstone.

In addition to being the first licensed aviator in North Carolina, Stewart is listed as the 221st licensed aviator in the United States.

For several seasons, Stewart was the only civilian Tar Heel licensed to fly. Many people traveled long distances to watch his flights and he performed at county fairs and similar celebrations. He often taught others to fly and had many eager pupils. According to a 1988 Raleigh *News & Observer* column by Dennis Rogers, it was on a teaching assignment that Stewart lost his life.

Stewart had come to Coats to give Worth Stephenson of Dunn an advanced flying lesson. Hugh Blalock, a cousin of Stephenson, asked to go along as a passenger, and the three men climbed aboard the plane.

According to one account, Stephenson was at the controls at takeoff. The plane circled the town of Coats and headed back to the field. It swooped low, then climbed. But during the climb, it suddenly flipped out of control and spiraled to the ground, killing all three men.

Three fatalities in a single day stunned the fledgling aviation community of North Carolina. When Stewart's body was carried to the Coats cemetery for burial, some of his fellow pilots flew their airplanes over the graveyard and dropped blossoms.

The outline of a pilot's face with helmet, goggles, and a scarf is engraved on Stewart's headstone. For many years, visitors could view his real likeness on a photograph embedded under plastic in the upper right corner of the granite marker, but vandals destroyed that and left a scarred oval.

Alfred Johnson of Fuquay-Varina, who as a youngster saw Stewart flying, has done considerable research on the aviator. He has even located a picture of Stewart and the Stewart family standing in front of the pilot's old bi-wing aircraft. Johnson and other history buffs have put together most of the facts of the pilot's life.

"We have been working toward having an historical marker erected in Stewart's honor and memory," said Johnson. "If we can't get approval for a highway marker, we can at least have a memorial plaque erected near either the crash site or the cemetery at Coats."

* * *

An airplane carved in stone commemorates the life and times of Austin Ray Perdue, who loved to fly above the high slopes and wooded valleys of Randolph County.

On the evening of July 14, 1982, when Daylight Saving Time lingered across the Uwharrie Mountains, Perdue was enjoying a flight over familiar terrain. An experienced pilot, he was trying out a one-seat ultralight aircraft. The engine failed, and Perdue crashed near his home in Farmer. He was fatally injured.

Perdue is buried in the cemetery at Science Hill Friends Meeting at the north end of Secondary Road 1142, just of N.C. Highway 49 in southwest Randolph County.

* * *

From a short distance away, it looks as if a child may have left a toy train atop Levi K. Matthews' tombstone. But closer inspection reveals that the train is made of granite. It is a replica of a locomotive and is part of the headstone.

Levi Matthews was a railroad man, and his monument confirms it:

In Active Service
With N&W Railway Co.
For 38 years, 4 mos.

He is buried near a railroad line at Salem Chapel on Secondary Road 1952 off U.S. Highway 311 in Forsyth County about three miles south of Walnut Cove.

Because of the proximity of the cemetery to the railroad, a passenger train stopped during Matthews' 1927 burial rites, and the train bell chimed along with the church bell to toll the mournful news. Matthews died at the age of 68, shortly after his retirement.

His was a storybook life, considering that he lived in an era when many boys hoped to grow up to be engineers on steam locomotives. As a young man, Matthews had worked for a short period at a West Virginia coal mine. A locomotive pulling coal cars at the mining area was a common sight.

A man who liked to tinker, Matthews often watched repairs being made on the locomotive owned by the coal company and listened to the "shop talk" of the mechanics. His curiosity and interest would hold him in good stead, although he didn't know it at the time.

Some years later, Matthews got a job with the Roanoke and Southern Railway, which later became part of the Norfolk & Western. He was part of a track gang, working with pick and shovel, toting rails. On a cold January day in 1889, while Matthews' crew was extending a track north of Winston-Salem, the locomotive of the work train broke down.

The trouble was diagnosed as a blown gasket. The crew couldn't continue without the train and its heavy equipment. When word of the work stoppage reached the railway office, the company president, Col. Francis H. Fries, came to the scene. Fries did some checking and found the nearest railway employee skilled in locomotive repair was stationed at Norfolk. To make matters worse, the mechanic wouldn't be able to get to the scene for nearly two weeks.

Col. Fries was at wit's end trying to get work back on schedule. It was then that Levi Matthews stepped forward and told Fries he would like to try his hand at repairing the locomotive. Fries said he would be more than grateful if Matthews could get the train running again. Indeed, Matthews was stunned by what Fries said would be his reward for success: he would be promoted to engineer the very minute he could get the train back on duty.

The locomotive was similar to the one Matthews had watched mechanics repairing in his coal mining days, and he soon had it huffing and puffing again. Good to his word, Col. Fries promoted him to engineer on the spot.

In an article in *The State* magazine in February, 1987, Herb Thompson wrote:

"Most engineers must spend a minumum of three years as a fireman before they become eligible for promotion to engineer and several years on a freight train before they ever put a hand on the throttle of a passenger train. But Mr. Matthews began his career as an engineer at the top of the seniority list, before the first passenger train on his division ever ran. And he spent the remaining years of his life until retirement with his his hand on the throttle of a passenger engine."

Matthews' usual run was between Winston-Salem, N.C., and Roanoke, Va. Thousands of people living along the route knew his friendly wave as he passed. When he died, his funeral was scheduled to take into account the time the passenger train usually passed the vicinity of the church. An arrangement was made with the Norfolk & Western Railroad for the train to stop for a two-minute period and have the engineer toll the train bell in remembrance.

Inside the church, the mourners sang a departing hymn: "Life Is Like a Mountain Railroad."

* * *

Linville W. Tilley was always fascinated by the clickety-clack of a train traveling over steel tracks. A resident of Summerfield in

A replica of a locomotive is carved into Levi K. Matthews' gravestone near Walnut Cove in Forsyth County.

Linville Tilley, buried at Westminster Gardens in Greensboro, also has a carved locomotive on his gravestone, as well as a coal car that serves as a flower container.

Guilford County, Tilley was a railroad man most of his life. His last duy before retirement was as a brakeman for Southern Railway.

When Tilley died in 1981 at 72, he was buried at Westminster Memorial Gardens on Westridge Road in Greensboro, where grave markers are level with the ground. His wife Edna and two daughters, Lona and Pauline, had his bronze grave plaque engraved with the outline of a small locomotive.

But that didn't seem enough to commemorate Tilley's pride and love for his work, so they commissioned Baxter Jones of Thomasville to build a model of a Southern Railway locomotive and coal car at the gravesite. Tilley's retirement year, 1961, is painted on the cab of the engine. The coal car serves as a flower container.

* * *

Buddy Clapp died on duty aboard a runaway train that went down in song and story. Millions of people came to know the name of the train, its engineer and the tragedy, but few people ever heard of its brave fireman, Albion G. Clapp, better known as Buddy. But his tombstone in Springwood Presbyterian Church Cemetery at Whitsett in eastern Guilford County makes it known that he was part of the story:

Killed In
Wreck No. 97
Danville, Va.
Sept. 27, 1903.

Old 97 was the crackerjack mail train that wrecked near Danville, killing its crew of five and six postal employees. Four of the 11 victims were Tar Heels: Clapp, the fireman from Whitsett; John M. Hodge, apprentice fireman of Raleigh; John T. Blair, conductor from Spencer; and James R. Moody, flagman from Raleigh.

The tragedy stirred a nation into mourning. A popular ballad told the epic story of the speeding train and efforts of the engineer and fireman to stop it. The sad tune is still played at fiddlers' conventions and sung at gatherings of country musicians:

They handed him his orders at Monroe, Virginia.
Saying 'Steve, you're way behind time.
This is not 38. this is old 97,
You must put 'er in Spencer on time...'

It's a mighty rough road from Lynchburg to Danville
And a line on a three-mile grade.
It was on that grade that he lost his air brake.
And you can see what a jump he made.

Speed was the pride of yesteryear's best-known trains, and being on time was the pride of the engineer and the railroad. But there was more. If a train also was a mail train, as Old 97 was, there was a penalty to pay the U.S. Postal Service if it got behind schedule.

There was nothing wrong with "pouring on a little more coal" when trains were behind schedule, but in this instance, the brakes of Old 97 apparently became defective at a critical time.

Like many other mail trains, Old 97 was so consistently on time that farmers along the route often checked their watches by its passing. But that day Old 97 was an hour late pulling out of Washington, D.C. When it arrived at Monroe, Va., it still hadn't gained any time. A new crew, with Steve Broady as engineer, took over at Monroe and sought to do something about that. By calling on his North Carolina fireman to keep the furnace stoked hot and the steam gauge high, Broady planned to make up as much lost time as he could.

He steamed into the open country toward Lynchburg, pushing the engine as he had done others. But Broady had never coaxed Old 97 before. He had made this run many times at the throttle of other engines, but 97 was to be his undoing.

Broady was impatient about stopping at Lynchburg because he would lose time, but the stop had to be on the record. Barely had the train come to a halt, though, before Broady began easing back the throttle again. It is said a railroad "safe locker" got on the train to perform his station check but did not finish in time and had to stay aboard.

Time was a-wasting as far as Broady was concerned, and he pushed that big engine faster and faster. When the train reached northern Danville, Broady learned a sickening fact. He could not slow down. The brakes had failed.

So Broady pulled the cord on the steam whistle and held it down as the train roared on. The continuous scream let all railroad people know that a runaway train was coming. The engineer and fireman managed to reverse the steam pistons but too late. Momentum was in charge.

The train failed to make a curve and left the tracks at the worst possible place, plunging off the 45-foot high Stillhouse Trestle, creating a mangled mass of fire and rubble below, a death trap for Buddy Clapp and 10 others.

A 33-year-old bachelor, Clapp had given up farming to be a fireman two years earlier. Ironically, he wasn't even supposed to have been working that day. In a 1984 *Greensboro News & Record* story, writer Conrad Paysour quoted Clapp's niece, Maude Crews of Greensboro, as saying her uncle had substituted for another fireman on that run. In 1989, Mrs. Crews, then 92, reiterated that story, saying family history has it that her uncle had volunteered to work for the regular fireman, who had taken off to get married, a favor that cost Clapp his life.

Old 97 didn't make it to "Spencer on time" that fateful day, but it did get there eventually. Weeks after the wreck, it was hoisted from the ravine and hauled to the famous Spencer Shops, now a railroad museum, where it was repaired and put back into service as engine No. 1102. It served nearly 30 more years before being scrapped in Indiana in 1930.

* * *

The steam locomotive, Engine No. 2046, engraved on Ray Jordan's granite tombstone at Oaklawn Cemetery in Asheboro in Randolph County, looks as if it might puff its way right off the monument.

Ernest Raymond Jordan of Asheboro never worked on trains or for a railroad, but the enchantment of the rails found its way into his blood, and he became a model railroader. The call of faraway places that beckoned Jordan, a mechanic, was satisfied by miniature trains and the trips they took around tiny tracks laid in various patterns in an outbuilding at his home.

"He had become interested in trains as a child, and he never lost it," said his mother, Gertrude Jordan. "All his years as a boy he bought trains, tracks, and parts for railways whenever he got spending money. Then, when he got old enough to work, he really began buying in earnest. Over the years he had many, many sets, some very fine outfits."

A brother, David, who in later years also became a model train buff, said, "Ray had model trains for years and years. He had them when he was a kid. He had them when he became a man. He had them after he got married. He had them when he died...."

Ray Jordan was 61 when died in June 1981, still loving trains as much as he did in boyhood.

* * *

The outline of a Klopman Mill tractor and trailer is carved not once but twice on the granite tombstone of Clyde York Surratt.

The rig is pictured on both front and back of Surratt's stone at Lineberry Methodist Church Cemetery at Handy, a small community along N.C. Highway 109 south of Denton in Davidson County. Surratt, who died in 1977, was employed in the transportation department of Klopman Mills at Asheboro.

* * *

A bulldozer is carved on the tombstone of James R. Cheek at St. Paul's Churchyard on High Point Street in Randleman in Randolph County. Cheek died in 1971 at 40.

* * *

A Harley-Davidson motorcycle is engraved on the tombstone of U. S. Marine veteran Charles T. Hill in Asheboro's city cemetery along U.S. Highway 64 in Randolph County. Beneath the bike is inscribed:

No man soars too high
If he soars with his own wings.
                        -C.T.

50

According to his obituary, Hill, 29, died from injuries received in an accident on August 25, 1978, after he lost control of his motorcycle near Pleasant Garden south of Greensboro.

* * *

A picture of a large motor home decorates the tombstone of Jessie Mae Boyd in Westwood Cemetery at Carrboro in Orange County. A beautician for nearly 50 years, Boyd and her husband, Clifton, enjoyed being on the road and staying at campsites.

"Jessie Mae liked living in our motor home as much, maybe more, than living in our regular home," Clifton said. "We had been to every continental state except Alaska, and we were going to go there the summer she died."

Jessie Mae had a heart attack in early 1971. She died June 7, just about the time the Boyds would have left for a summer of new adventure in Alaska.

* * *

Charles L. Britt was a farmer who loved the rural life. So, when he died in May, 1985, and was buried at the town cemetery in Candor on U.S. Highway 220 in Montgomery County, a rural scene was put upon his stone, including his favorite tractor and three chickens scratching the ground.

* * *

Percy O. Leggett was a volunteer fireman at Southport in Brunswick County for 44 years, 24 of those years as chief. When he died in 1977 at 61, his family had a fire engine and a fireman's badge engraved on his headstone at the town's Old Burying Ground.

* * *

A 1960, 861 Ford diesel tractor is carved on the tombstone of Marvin Bescher, a successful farmer who lived near Jackson Creek in Randolph County.

"My grandfather had farm machinery before that model, of course," said his grandson Wayne Bescher, "but when he bought that

Motorized vehicles are on several graves in North Carolina. Top, the grave of Jessie Mae Boyd in Orange County; Center, the grave of Percy O. Leggett in Brunswick County; Bottom, the grave of Charles T. Hill in Randolph County.

52

More vehicles: Top, the grave of
Marvin Bescher in Randolph County;
Center, the grave of James R. Cheek,
also in Randolph County; Bottom, the
grave of Edward L. Poe in Moore
County.

tractor it was one of the first diesel models in this part of the country. He was proud of that tractor until the day he died."

He died in September of 1961 and was buried at Bend Cemetery a half mile north of his farm.

"We found the owner's manual that had come with the tractor, and it had a picture of that model in it," his grandson said. "The stone cutter used that copy in engraving the tractor on my grandfather's headstone."

* * *

Edward L. Poe, a 29-year-old used car dealer in Moore County, was killed when he wrecked his Corvette on September 14, 1985. Both his Corvette and the name of his business, Poe's Used Cars, were engraved on his tombstone at Pine Rest Cemetery along Old Park Road at Robbins.

Murder Took Them to the Grave

The three Hulin Brothers of Montgomery County did not want to fight in the Civil War. Conscientious objectors, they hid out but were found and executed for evading miltary duty.

On their joint tombstone at Lovejoy Church, northwest of the county seat of Troy, is an unmistakable word engraved in their memory:

Murdered.

When the Civil War broke out in 1861, thousands of Tar Heel men rallied to the cause. But many hundreds also felt conscience-bound not to take part in killing. Among those whose allegiance was to a higher authority were Elisha Moore and his brother-in-law, Jessie Hulin, as well as Jessie's two brothers, John and William. When conscription became the law in the spring of 1862, the Hulin brothers refused to be drafted because of their beliefs and went into hiding.

They were characterized by the pro-war factions as "liers-out" or "outliers," a name given to those men who hid in the woods near their homes and avoided capture and punishment by the Home Guard, or "Rebels" as they were frequently called in Montgomery County.

According to an article by Thoburn M. Freeman in *The Heritage of Montgomery County*, Montgomery County Historical Society, 1981, Elisha Moore was stricken with pneumonia. He was secretly visited in his wilderness hideout by his wife and his sister-in-law, Caroline Hulin, who nursed him and administered homemade, herbal medicines. He recovered and was successful in staying hidden the rest of the war.

The Hulin Brothers were not so lucky. Although they stayed hidden most of the war years by surviving on wilderness fare and food brought under darkness by their kin, fate intervened. Just four months before the Confederates surrendered in the spring of 1865, the Hulin brothers were found by authorities at their Buck Mountain hideout and executed.

Who shot them is not known, but among officers in charge were Aaron Saunders and Watt Zigler.

The brothers, Jessie, 34, John, 24, and William, 22, were buried at Lovejoy Churchyard. The graveyard is along Secondary Road 1315, which winds through the Uwharrie Mountains on the edge of the Uwharrie National Forest.

* * *

Wong Bow's epitaph is in Chinese.

Born in 1882, Wong was shot to death at his laundry at Wadesboro in Anson County on April 23, 1927. He was well liked by the townspeople, and his death, the details of which are now lost, shocked the small town. Few people in Wadesboro remember him now, but Harvey Leavitt Jr., of Leavitt Funeral Home does.

"Would you believe it if I told you I still have the original cardboard grave marker that my father put on Mr. Bow's grave as a temporary identification?" Leavitt asked. "The cardboard started to weather away before a permanent stone was put up. When a regular tombstone was erected, I brought that little piece of weatherbeaten cardboard back here, and it is still in this desk drawer, over 50 years later!"

Leavitt fished around among some loose papers in the old desk and located it.

"I was young, of course, when Mr. Bow was murdered," he said. "I never heard anything about his wife, whether she had died or was still in China, or what. I never knew anything about the family other than that Mr. Bow had a son, Tom."

After his father's death, Tom was befriended by a prominent Wadesboro family who reared him.

"Tom attended and graduated from Wake Forest College," said Hewitt. "Then, I was told, he operated a restaurant. It seems I

WONG BOW
1882 — 1927

黃保廷墳墓

終於民國十六年四月廿三号

廣東台山縣海口华東姜村

Wong Bow's gravestone is one of the few in North Carolina engraved in Chinese. He is buried in Anson County.

remember something about him serving in the army in World War II and serving in the Pacific, even went to China. I think he lives in Atlanta now. Once in a long, long while I see him here in Wadesboro driving through town. A trip back here once every few years is kind of a nostalgia thing as well as a chance to visit his dad's grave. At least that's what he told me on one of his trips."

Wong's grave is in the town cemetery bounded by Brent, East View, and Lilesville Streets, just inside the Brent Street entrance. His tombstone is one of the few in North Carolina engraved with Chinese characters. Translated, the stone reads:

Died 1927, April 23.

Gravestone of Wong Bow.

Canton State
White Mountain City
Oceanside
East County.

* * *

Tom Dooley's epitaph does not have kind things to say for him:

Hanged For The Murder Of
Laura Foster.

And Laura Foster's tombstone, several miles away, makes sure everyone knows she was the victim:

Murdered In May 1865.
Tom Dula Hanged For Crime.

Laura Foster was fatally stabbed by her boyfriend Tom Dooley (as mountain people pronounced Dula) in Wilkes County in 1866 (the 1865 date on her tombstone is in error). Or so said the courts.

The murder became one of the most famous in North Carolina history, heralded by an old mountain ballad that was spread by

58

At left, the grave of Laura Foster, said to be murdered by Tom Dula (Dooley), whose grave is pictured below. Both are in Wilkes County.

country singers at fiddlers' conventions. In 1958, the popular Kingston Trio made a national hit of their own version of the song, incorporating the old refrain of the Brushy Mountain troubadours:

Hang down your head, Tom Dooley.
Hang down your head and cry....

Tom Dooley was a handsome young man who caught the eyes of several young women in Wilkes County. His choice was Ann Foster. But the Civil War was afoot. Dooley went off to fight and was captured. Ann didn't wait for him. She became a Melton by marriage.

When Dooley returned home three years later, he began to date Laura Foster. But he carried on a secret affair with Ann, while promising to marry Laura. On the day they were to wed, Laura rode off on horseback to meet Tom and disappeared. Her body was found in a shallow grave on a mountain ridge a few weeks later.

Rumors spread that Ann Foster Melton was involved. She was said to be very jealous. Some thought that she might have met the bridal couple on the mountain and stabbed Laura during an argument.

Dooley fled but was captured and maintained his innocence. Defended in court by famed Zeb Vance, who later became governor of North Carolina, he was convicted on circumstantial evidence and rode to his execution in a wagon sitting atop his coffin.

"My grandfather and some other relatives went to Dooley's hanging down at Statesville in 1868," said Lawrence Winkler, an area resident who sometimes leads visitors to Laura Foster's grave. "My grandfather said he heard Dooley's last statement before a black hood was put over Dooley's head and a rope adjusted around his neck. Dooley told the crowd, 'I didn't touch a hair of that girl's head, but maybe I deserve this.' They understood that to mean he must've known a good deal about the murder.

"Laura Foster worked for my grandmother, weaving and also helping around the house. My grandmother Mary thought well of her. She said Laura's mother had died when Laura was quite small. When Laura's father told my grandfather, Walter Winkler, that he had no place to bury Laura, my grandfather told him to go down there in the field near the Yadkin River and bury her there."

The grave is a lone mound in a cow pasture on the south side of

N.C. Highway 268, just across the Caldwell County line.

"It has these wooden slats around it to keep the cows off it," said Winkler as he stood by the grave. "She is buried way out here, away from town, because her father didn't own any land...My grandfather donated the gravesite. The land has changed hands over the years though. It is now owned by three brothers who live near Deep Gap."

Tom Dooley is buried about three miles northeast. His grave, too, is a lonely mound in an old pasture atop a bank along Secondary Road 1134, east of where N.C. Highway 268 meets the Yadkin River at Ferguson. In 1987, the state erected a highway historical marker calling attention to the grave.

Dooley's tombstone has frequently been vandalized by souvenir hunters who have chipped off hunks. Laura Foster's tombstone was stolen in 1986 and was found discarded a year later behind a Caldwell County dumpster and returned.

Even today, people in the Yadkin Valley of the Brushy Mountains still talk about the murder of Laura Foster as if it happened "not long ago." Many still feel that Ann Melton killed Laura and that Dooley went silently to the gallows for her.

A story is told that on her deathbed many years later, Ann confessed to her family doctor. He never betrayed that confidence, but he indicated that he believed Dooley innocent.

* * *

A little noted tombstone at Carthage in Moore County carries this intriguing epitaph:

The Grave of
Stephen
Son Of Stephen and Jane Davis
Wounded
Near Scuffletown, Robeson Co., N.C.
Oct. 4, 1870
Died
Oct. 10, 1870

Promptly answering to the voice of duty,
He fell a sacrifice for the public good.
A victim to the violence of the
Lowery Banditti.

Scuffletown is now the town of Pembroke in Robeson County (the old name survives in the Scuffletown Fire District, which surrounds the town), but the tomb of Stephen Davis is 60 miles away at Carthage United Methodist Church on McReynolds Street.

Scuffletown was the center of an area populated by a large group of Indians who later came to be known as Lumbees. Following the Civil War, violence flared between whites and Indians in the area, including the vigilante lynching of Indians accused of minor crimes.

Henry Berry Lowrie's father and brother were executed for an alleged theft, and he vowed to fight back. In 1864, he led a band of Indians into the swamps from which they could strike at the vigilantes, and eight years of terror followed as they sought retribution, often raiding stores and depots for supplies and money. At least 10 deaths were attributed to Lowrie's band, including that of a former sheriff, but some believe many more were killed and injured.

Local authorities called Lowrie and his men "swamp outlaws" and sent posses to chase them. Stephen Davis was riding with one of those posses when he was shot on October 4, 1870. He died six days later. According to *To Die Game: The Story of the Lowry Band, Indian Guerrillas of Reconstruction,* by W. McKee Evans, Louisiana State University Press, 1971, Davis was among a 20-man posse that encountered Lowrie and 15 of his men at a farmhouse near Long Swamp. Lowrie's band fled into the swamp in a hail of gunfire. The posse pursued, only to be ambushed. With twilight nearing, the posse regrouped on a nearby knoll and discovered one of their members wounded, another missing. The missing man was Stephen Davis.

A scouting party found Davis seriously wounded. Although nearby pools of blood indicated that some of Lowrie's men were also wounded, the posse captured none. In following months, however, the band was captured a few at a time, each tried and sentenced. One, Henderson Oxendine, was indicted for the murder of Stephen Davis, tried, and executed only 19 days after his capture. Others in the band were sentenced to hang but none ever did.

Lowrie escaped from a Wilmington jail and was never recaptured. He reportedly died in 1872 after accidentally shooting himself, but his body was never found.

Lowrie's name is now spoken with pride in Robeson County, where many Indians consider him a hero. Two books and numerous articles about him have been published, and an outdoor drama based on his life, *Strike At The Wind*, is produced annually.

Safe Ports or Watery Graves

An epitaph on the marble gravestone of Captain Lewis Lee (March 17, 1787-December 5, 1855) in Cedar Grove Cemetery at New Bern reminds landlubbers of the origins of the seas:

They that go down to the sea in ships;
That do business in great waters;
These see the works of the Lord
And His wonders in the deep.

* * *

Another seafaring man is buried in the same graveyard at George and Queen Streets at the head of tidewater Neuse River in Craven County. Captain William Harker survived perilous seas only to fall ill to a fever while on shore. He was only 32 when he died in 1822. His epitaph eloquently tells how his life came to an end:

The form that fills this stilly grave
Once toss'd on the ocean's roaring wave,
Plunged through its storms without dismay
And careless whirled in its spray;
Wreck, famine, exile, scatheless bore
Yet perished on this peaceful shore,
No tempest whelm'd him neath the surge;
No wailing seabird scream'd his dirge;
But Fever's silent, hidden flame
Consum'd by stealth his hardy frame

And softly as an infant's breath
He sank into the arms of Death.
The weatherbeaten Bark no more
Hangs shivering on a leeward shore
But wafted by a favouring wind
Life's stormy sea hath left behind
And into ports securely pass'd
Hath dropped its anchor here at last.

* * *

The reference to dropping anchor also appears on the grave of Captain John Hill in Beaufort's Old Burying Ground. Hill died in 1879 at 62. His son put these words on his marker:

The form that fills this silent grave
Once tossed on ocean rolling wave,
But in a port securely fast
Has dropped his anchor here at last.

* * *

The nearby sea has taken many other lives as other tombstones at the old cemetery attest:

Henry Gilbert
"Ordinary seaman"
Drowned
June 1895.

* * *

Captain John Hill's gravestone in Beaufort's Old Burying Ground is one of several that refers to dropping anchor.

When the waters off North Carolina's coast get angry, ships, cargo, and people are swallowed, sometimes never to be seen again. If lifeless bodies do get tossed back on the beach, the ordeals of the victims are recalled in local legends and noted in epitaphs at coastal cemeteries.

This monument is erected
By many citizens who regret
The untimely death
Of these pilots
Who in the faithful
Discharge of their DUTY
Were suddenly called
To meet
Their God.

The winds and the sea
Sing their requiem
And shall forevermore.

So states a monument at Southport Cemetery in Brunswick County. It is dedicated to those men who lost their lives while piloting ships in the dangerous Cape Fear waters. Among the names carved in stone are Brinkman, Bensea, Sellers, George, Trout, Grissom, Walker, Gillespie, Dosher, and Piner.

Emaline Taylor lost her life on Christmas Eve:

Swept from the upper deck
Of Steamer
San Francisco
Dec . 24, 1853.

* * *

When James Pettigrew was 11, his family's longtime physician

67

told his parents to send him on an ocean cruise to improve his puny health. Some advice. During a storm at sea, the boy was swept overboard and drowned.

His mossy marker in the tiny family cemetery at the end of Secondary Road 1181 east of Somerset Place State Historic Site on the Tyrrell and Washington County lines tells a story of triumph:

> *Drown'd in the Atlantic from on*
> *board the ship 'Waverly' while on a*
> *voyage from New York to Mobile for his*
> *health, Oct. 27. 1833. Aged 11 years,*
> *8 months and 29 days.*

> *Young voyager oe'r life's tempestuous sea,*
> *It's waves have not one terror left for thee.*
> *Calm as the cradled infant's is thy sleep*
> *Of hushed repose, beneath the dark blue deep;*
> *Through all the wait of vast ocean rest*
> *In restless depth, upon thy gentle breast.*
> *At the archangel's trumpet thy chainless soul*
> *Shall burst the floods that oe'r thee roll.*
> *And in his might, who triumped oe'r grave*
> *With angel pinions cleave astonished waves.*

Bits and Pieces

Tar Heels visiting England may wish to look for an odd epitaph in Banbury Cemetery. Richard Richards suffered two surgical amputations only to die of gangrene. This is engraved on his tombstone:

To the memory of Richard Richards.
Who by gangrene lost first a toe,
Afterwards a leg, and lastly his life
On the 7th of April, 1656.

Ah cruel Death,
To make three meals of one,
To taste and taste
Till all was gone.
But know, then Tyrant,
When the trumpet shall call,
He'll find his feet and stand
When thou shall fall.

It is not known if Richards' toe and leg were honored with separate burials and given their own epitaphs. But North Carolina has three documented interments of limbs with engraved markers.

James A. Reid lost his foot to a freight train on November 25, 1893. It is buried at the southwest corner wall of the Lutheran Cemetery in Salisbury.

Sugg's Creek Cemetery in northern Montgomery County has a similar grave:

ARM OF JESSE MANESS

The arm was buried July 9, 1913. Maness did not follow it to the grave until 1969. In the interim, Maness sometimes stopped by the spot where his arm was buried, and each time he shook his head about an error on the marker.

"He pointed out the stone to me many times in our early years," said his wife, Esther, before her death in 1989. "'Look,' he'd say, 'They got the wrong arm carved on it. They marked the stone with the outline of a left arm, but it is my right arm that is buried there.' But he always said he was going to let it go, and he did. He didn't raise a fuss about it."

Jesse was 12 when he got his sleeve tangled in a sawmill and lost his arm. But he never let the handicap bother him. He continued operating sawmills, became a storekeeper, and farmed 1,500 acres. He was a legendary figure in his small community, and his store on Secondary Road 1349 was a center of community life.

"Jesse put the first TV set known in these parts in that country store..." his wife said. "People came from all over...They came all hours, but especially at night. I loved the store too, and loved the people, but do you know, they got so thick it was almost aggravating at times. Jesse loved boxing and wrestling matches and had them on the set all the time. That was back in '52. We didn't even have a TV set in the house."

When Jesse Maness died of a blood ailment at 68, he was taken to the same cemetery as his arm. But there was no room near his lost appendage, and he was buried about 10 graves away.

* * *

When Frank Webster's arm was injured in a farm accident and amputated in 1966, it was buried at Sapling Ridge Church Cemetery in northern Chatham County.

Eleven years later, in 1977, a stone marker was put at the spot.the

Webster's Arm

Above, a stone marks the spot where arm of Jesse Maness is buried in Montgomery County. At left, Jesse Maness and his wife, Esther.

On the same day that flat marker was embedded in the ground, a headstone was also erected at a new grave alongside it for Webster, who had died a few weeks earlier, on July 5.

"I thought that while having a stone put at my husband's grave, it would be proper to have one made for his arm that he is buried next to," said his widow, Lessie Lindley Webster.

Webster's brother-in-law, Harry Perry, recalled how Webster lost his arm at 62.

"Frank and I were at the combine, which had just been put into idle, and I started to walk away to pick up something. I heard Frank holler, and I looked back. His hand, wrist and lower arm were in the combine. I ran back and cut the combine off. Then I ran to my toolbox, grabbed a long screwdriver, came back, and shoved it down into the shaft and gears and began to turn 'em back little by little until Frank's arm was free. I told him to sit down and wait right there, I'd run to the house for towels and stuff to wrap up his arm, and I'd drive him quickly to the doctor or hospital. Before I could get back to him, he was coming across the field, halfway to the house by himself."

"I'll never, ever, forget that day," Mrs. Webster said. "I had been sitting out by the well, sewing sacks, when I heard the hum of of the combine stop and I wondered why...In a few minutes a car drove into the yard and a niece, Jeanette Phillip, ran to to me and said 'Uncle Frank's been hurt. Come with us to the hospital.' They had to amputate Frank's arm just above the right elbow. In a day or two, after some of the shock wore off, they asked Frank what he wanted done with his arm. He said, 'Bury it at Sapling Ridge Cemetery.' And they did. Frank healed quickly and got right back to farming. It was always said he was as good a worker, as good a hand as any man on any farm crew anywhere. He was, too.

"He insisted on doing everything for himself, if he could possibly figure out a way, no matter how hard. About the only thing he couldn't master was to button that one shirt sleeve. He'd even take that button in his teeth and try to thread it through the hole! I remember he once said, right after he came home from the hospital, that he might not ever again be able to draw a bucket of water from well and bring it to me. But one day he went out there, turned the windlass with his one hand, and brought a bucket up full of water. I

The marker for Frank Webster's arm, buried in Chatham County.

just watched to to see what he would do next. How could he hold the windlass with his one hand and then remove the bucket from the hook too? Well, he just tucked the handle of that windlass between his legs and held it to free his hand. Then he lifted the bucket free. A big smile came across his face. You see, he just wouldn't let anything lick him. Why, he even learned how to tie his shoes with one hand!"

This monument, erected by the volunteer firemen of Charlotte, salutes firemen everywhere.

Tough Jobs

A monument to often unsung heroes stands in Elmwood Cemetery at Charlotte. Although the massive marble marker was erected in memory of local volunteer firemen, it pays homage to all volunteer firefighters because of the statue atop it. Crowned with a steel fire helmet and holding an axe, the figure represents all firefighters.

The monument was erected October 10, 1883, by the volunteer firemen of Charlotte as a lasting tribute to their dead comrades. It is a short distance inside the cemetery's West 6th Street gate, about 100 feet along the first left fork in the road.

The sides of the monument are engraved:

Fire Department Organized
Oct. 10, 1883

Independence Hook And ladder Company
Organized Aug. 4, 1868

Pioneer Fire Company
Organized May 20, 1874

Hornet Fire Company Organized
Organized Jan. 29, 1867.

* * *

Thousands of war veterans are buried in Tar Heel soil, and many have long, well-deserved eulogies carved upon their stones. But a brief epitaph on the headstone of Mickey M. Hopkins at New Hope Church Cemetery in Randolph County would do honors to all:

In grateful memory
Of a brave soldier
Who gave his life
In defense of his country.
Soldier rest.
Thy work is done.

Hopkins died September 23, 1918, during World War I.

* * *

One side of the double tombstone under which Henry Willis Jr. is buried in Sunset Cemetery at Shelby in Cleveland County is engraved with a picture of an automobile generator. The other side depicts a hairbrush and comb carved in crossed-swords fashion.

"They represent my occupation," Faye Willis said, explaining the comb and hairbrush. "When Henry died and I decided to put an auto generator emblem on the stone to represent the work he did all his life, I thought I might just as well put my beauty parlor tools on there too."

Henry Willis had an auto generator and starter repair shop at his home for 32 years until two heart attacks ended his career. He died in 1976 at 65.

When Faye Willis first told the stone cutter to copy a picture of a car generator and a brush and comb on the family tombstone, he was doubtful about the outcome.

"But when it was finished, he felt the designs were fantastic," Mrs. Willis said. "He told me he even took his wife to the cemetery to show her how well the carvings came out."

* * *

A complicated knitting machine is engraved on the headstone of Jack B. Small Sr. at Tabernacle Church Cemetery along Secondary Road 1344 in western Randolph County. But to Small, such machines

76

were simple. He spent most of his life working with them, first in an Asheboro mill, then in his own business.

"He put a couple of knitting machines in the basement of the house," his son Rick recalled. "Then, when he got started good, he traded some land he owned at the beach for more knitting machines."

In 1971, Small created a little factory by remodeling a long-closed store that had belonged to his grandparents, Frank and Minnie Gallimore, and operated it as J.B. Small Hosiery Mill. When he died in 1986, family members felt the carving of an old Banner-style knitting machine would best exemplify the love he had for his work.

* * *

By the sweat of his brow and the brawn of his muscles, Claude Jerome Seabolt did his duty until he died at 68. He is buried at New Hope Methodist Church Cemetery in Randolph County. The words on his tombstone give him a belated pat on the back:

A well-deserved rest
For a hard worker.

* * *

No inscription is needed at the grave of Fletcher Stout to let the passersby know his occupation.

A millstone from his water-powered grist mill on Richland Creek marks his grave at Shiloh Christian Church Cemetery along Secondary Road 2895 west of Coleridge in Randolph County.

* * *

In life, Sandra Lynn Williams Klock was involved with real estate. But when life was over, her claim to land was no greater than for those who had gone before her: a small cemetery plot.

Sandra L. W. Klock, once of Asheboro in Randolph County, died November 25, 1979 at Pueblo, Colorado, at 33. She was president-elect of the Pueblo Board of Realtors. On her tombstone at Dover

At right, the grave of Sandra Klock, which shows her designation as a Realtor. The grave is in Moore County. Below, the tombstone for Henry Willis Jr., who owned an automobile generator and starter repair shop, and for his wife, Faye, who is a beautician.

Cemetery in north Moore County is a large, black, stylized "R" in a square, the logo for Realtor.

An old world adage is carved upon her stone:

May the road rise to greet you
May the rain fall softly on your fields
And until we meet again
May you be gently held in the hand of God.

Sweet, Sweet Music

A fiddle is engraved on one end of John S. Vuncannon's double tombstone, while a piano graces the the other end, the resting place of his beloved wife Addie Lassiter. Addie died in 1947. John followed her to the grave a year later. Their marker at Science Hill Friends Cemetery in Randolph County often brings the comment:

They made sweet music together.

* * *

Sweet music is also the legacy of Pearl Frick of the Liberty community of Rowan County. Her epitaph in the churchyard along Secondary Road 1004 recalls it:

Remembering her
Is as sweet and inspiring
As the music she loved.

* * *

There can be little doubt that Lynnie J. Johnson of Chatham County loved music. A musical scale is engraved upon her stone at Asbury United Methodist Church Cemetery at the junction of Secondary Roads 2151 and 2152 along with the words:

Whispering Hope.

That was the title of her favorite hymn. Lynnie Johnson, who died in 1987, sang in the church choir. "She had a beautiful alto voice," said a friend, Hilda Stout.

* * *

A dulcimer is carved on the headstone of T. A. "Tom" Cox at Shiloh Christian Church Cemetery on Secondary Road 2895 west of Coleridge in southeastern Randolph County. Cox (1883-1961) not only knew how to play the old-timey stringed instruments, he also taught himself to make them.

The late Vaughn Marley, a longtime local columnist, once wrote of Cox that "...he played such an instrument from childhood through life and loved it above all his hobbies."

* * *

An organ is pictured on the tombstone of LaRue A. Copple at Science Hill Friends Cemetery along Secondary Road 1107 northeast of Farmer in Randolph County. Copple, a music teacher, was music and choir director of the church. Upon her death in 1985, the LaRue Copple Music Fund was established at the Meeting.

* * *

Picking a tune on a guitar was a talent that Baxter F. Rummage, Jr., admired. When he died at 55 in 1979, he was buried at Reeds Baptist Church Cemetery on N.C. Highway 150 at Secondary Road 1192 in Davidson County, and a guitar and a few musical notes were carved on his headstone.

* * *

The guitar carved on the headstone of Jesse Franklin Hopkins at Barbeque Church along N.C. 27 in western Harnett County is large and deeply etched in the granite.

Hopkins, who was born in 1942 and died in 1983, was known as Jack to family and friends. He not only played guitar but also composed songs.

A guitar is carved into the headstone of Jesse Franklin Hopkins, who is buried in Harnett County.

"Jack played base guitar in a country band," said his mother, Betty Hopkins. "He wrote many poems and songs. I well remember the day he wrote the one we had engraved on his tombstone. He came to me and said, 'Momma, I wrote you a poem.' It was written on just an old scrap piece of paper. I read it and told him I liked it, that it was beautiful. He said, 'If you like it so much, I'll have it put on something worth keeping.' A few days later he came back and handed me a framed, white silken cloth with those nice words neatly written upon it."

A sister, Hazel Meyer, recalled that "Jack had been interested in music all his life. He eventually played with a country band called Felony. He was interested in writing poetry and wrote many verses, but he also wrote two copyrighted songs."

When Jack Hopkins died from complications of diabetes, his family remembered the poem he wrote for his mother and had it engraved on his tombstone. It begins:

> *Life is love, as we can see,*
> *But without it, what would there be.*

Heavenly Doctors
and Fitful Fevers

The words carved on the grave marker of Dr. Neilson Coppedge at Candor Town Cemetery are a spiritual tombstone tonic:

Office Now Up Stairs.

A country doctor, Coppedge served patients in the peach growing area known as the Sandhills. He died in 1943 at 63, but he is still revered in Moore, Montgomery, and Richmond Counties, where he spanked some 3,000 babies into life,

"He really cared about people," said his nephew, William W. Coppedge of Raleigh, who lived with him from childhood. "I remember a black man came to him once, driving up alone in a horse and wagon. The man had been snake bitten and was in no condition to be doing his own driving. Dr. Coppedge doctored the man and then took him home—drove him home in an automobile. He was that kind of man.

"He also kept patients on a cot at the office or at his home for several days sometimes, if it were necessary, to keep a close eye on them. I later saw his records, his books, and they were truly a revelation as to the relationship he had with his patients. They often couldn't pay him cash, and records show they paid with produce, chickens, even buckets of blueberries and blackberries they had picked. A nickel looked as big as a wagon wheel to them back in the Depression."

Dr. Coppedge was born in the summer of 1880 in Richmond County. By 1909, he was postmaster at Ellerbe, serving until 1914. Then medicine called. His grades in college and medical school remained the highest on record for many decades. He practiced in Biscoe for a few years, then moved to Candor. Tall, balding, and bespectacled, Dr. Coppedge was truly an "oldtimey country doctor." He made house calls, and people also came to his home as well as to his office, day and night.

"He was outgoing in many respects," his nephew recalled. "He wore a necktie and business suit, but he didn't like formal attire or fancy cars. He always drove plain-looking Fords and Chevrolets."

Dr. Coppedge also liked "to play chess and even take part in those old-fashioned spelling bees," said his nephew, "and I never saw him stumped. I'd hear him quoting Shakespeare often. He frequently read Kipling and other authors to me. He read the Bible a lot and could quote it. I always felt he was a genius in his own way, but then I may have been a bit prejudiced....I remember when we'd go to homecoming at Macedonia Church, he said more than once, as we walked through the cemetery, that he liked the 'tree trunk' design tombstone he had noted occcasionally. He mused he might like to have a similar type for his last resting place.

"When that time did come, I tried to find a stone like that but never could. But the very next best thing, I thought, was something symbolic of Dr. Coppedge's feeling and thoughts about Jesus being a healer, The Great Physician, and that he'd tried to follow Christ in that respect. So, when he was buried, I thought it appropriate to mark his grave with the inscription: 'Office Now Up Stairs.' "

* * *

Aches and pains do not leave upon the death of those who were afflicted with them. Some remain, chiseled in stone:

Sick and sore she longtime bore.
Physicians were in vane;
Until God pleased to give her ease
And freed her from her pain.

Mary Cross was 59 when she died in 1909, leaving her pains behind. She was buried at Franklinville Baptist Church Cemetery on Church Street at Franklinville in Randolph County.

* * *

Robert Palmer's wife stayed sick all the time. The weather in the New World did not agree with her and caused ailments, she said. She took a ship back to the Old World, hoping to regain her health. It didn't do any good.

She returned to North Carolina and died, leaving her story in stone:

Here Lyes the body
Of
Margaret Palmer.
Who departed this life
Oct. 19. 1765
Age 44
After labouring ten of them
Under the severest of
Bodily afflictions
Brought on by
Change of climate;
And tho' she went to
Her native land
Receiv'd no relief
But returned where she bore them
With uncommon resolution,
And Resignation
To the last.

Margaret Palmer is buried at St. Thomas Episcopal Church at Bath, in Beaufort County, but not in the church cemetery. She was interred inside, under the floor of the sanctuary, where she never again had to be exposed to North Carolina's climate. Her tombstone is vertically embedded in the church wall to the right of the altar.

Edna Ferber, who came to Bath to research her novel *Show Boat* used Margaret Palmer's epitaph, with a change of name and age, in her book.

* * *

For a man who apparently suffered ill health, Balaam Mavey lived a long life. He was 83 when he died and was buried in the graveyard at Cane Creek Friends Meeting at Snow Camp in Alamance County. The quote on his tombstone tells his plight:

> *After life's fitful fever,*
> *He sleeps well.*

* * *

John W. R. Reece (1868-1913) thought birth and death were fair enough in their ways. Even so, he would have liked to have had more than the 45 years given him. His tombstone at Liberty town cemetery in Randolph County eloquently states his case:

> *In love he lived,*
> *In peace he died.*
> *His life was crav'd.*
> *But God denied.*

* * *

Ollie F. Leach was only 26 when she closed her eyes for all time. When she was buried in 1914 in Troy's town cemetery in Montgomery County, her brief epitaph explained:

> *God's Finger Touched Her*
> *And She Slept.*

* * *

The 'Office Now Up Stairs' for Dr. Neilson Coppedge, buried in Montgomery County

Inscribed on the gravestone of Dr. P.T. Beeman: 'I Fed Fever.'

Sarah J. Handley left home to attend Carolina Female College in Anson County. Established by a state charter in 1850, the Methodist college drew students from all over the South, but lost many of its students in its early years to three epidemics, one of measles and two of typhoid fever. Sarah Handley died there at 16 in 1852 of typhoid. It is said that she wrote her own epitaph before her death.

It can be found on her mossy marble tombstone at Bethlehem Cemetery off U.S. Highway 52 in Ansonville.

The pursuit of education
Led me from home,
I bade companions farewell
I met the contagion
And sunk to the tomb
And now with my Saviour
I dwell.
Our Union, how sweet,
Forever remains
Death parting
And sorrow is o' er.
The tempest may howl
And loud thunders roll,
Or the world
Into atoms be riven,
Yet calm are the feelings
That rest in my soul
There is nothing firmer
But Heaven.

* * *

Doc Beeman shifted weakly on his deathbed and told his family that he wanted them to be sure to put "I Fed Fever" on his tombstone. Dr. Parks Turner Beeman died at 70 in 1903 and was buried in the small family graveyard near Peachland in Anson County.

The engraving on his footstone does indeed carry his claim to fame:

I FED FEVER.

Practicing in the Civil War period, Doc Beeman had to make many decisions at a time when medical science knew little about some illnesses. He didn't mind being a maverick and trying his own methods if he saw the standard treatments of the time were not giving good results.

One of the standby adages of those days was to "Feed a cold and starve a fever." Doc Beeman challenged that. A feverish person is weak as it is, without making him suffer malnutrition, too, he figured. Let 'em eat, he always said. On one occasion, when a fever-ridden woman craved sauerkraut, he told the family to feed it to her.

There were, of course, those in the medical community who shook their heads at Doc Beeman's insistence on doing things his way. But Dr. Beeman was a rugged individualist, a man who not only acted but also frankly told folks what he thought.

Dr. Beeman was born in Wadesboro December 4, 1833. Little is known of his early life, but as a young man he "read" medicine under Dr. Edmund F. Ashe of Wadesboro. He completed his courses at Charleston Medical College and set up his medical practice at Peachland, which at that time was called Mulchai.

Pictures remain of Dr. Beeman showing his long beard and stern expression, a clue to his fierce independence. Below that austere countenance was a heart that reached out for "common folks," whom he often doctored whether they could pay or not. But woe be to bureaucrats and politicians who got in Doc Beeman's way or thought they were above reproach.

Dr. Beeman was opposed to the Civil War and said so. "Jeff Davis and secession should be in Hell where secession originated," he said early in the conflict. For uttering such blasphemy, he was arrested by Confederate troops and jailed at Camp Holmes near Raleigh, far from his beloved Anson County. Even in prison, his voice would not be stilled. He wrote many letters, making such statements as "We are treated like cattle," explaining prisoners were left out in the rain without tent or sheds. When Doc Beeman finally got a hearing and was released, he scorned assistance and walked all the way home, a distance of 140 miles.

After the war, Dr. Beeman went back to Raleigh, this time as an honored legislator. He spent two years there as a state senator representing the 29th District. Even then he punctured inflated egos. Among other things, he opposed a so-called "Militia Bill," saying it was an insult to the civil powers of the state.

After seeing and experiencing a large number of time-wasting operations conducted by the solons, he drew up a facetious bill asking a joint house and senate committee be appointed to study the feasibility of building or leasing space for an insane asylum as chambers for the entire North Carolina Legislature. Even though Doctor Beeman seemed to have a recalitrant attitude toward politics, authorities thought so highly of him that when his term was up, Raleigh officials asked him to stay as official physician for the capital city.

Twice he had been away from home, once in jail and once in the legislature. He would leave Anson County no more, he said. He went back to his Peachland home and got out his little black bag to be the doctor he was meant to be.

In the mid-to-late 1800s, when dengue and typhoid fever were among the plagues of the countryside, it was general medical practice to give liquids or nothing more solid than mashed potatoes to patients with those diseases. Doc Beeman scoffed at that. If a patient wanted meat and vegetables, let him have it, he said. And, surprisingly, many of his patients sucessfully fought off their illnesses.

He had other controversial treatments as well. One of his eight children, Blanche, was vastly underweight at birth. He kept her alive by giving her a few drops of liquor each day, along with any other nourishment the child would take.

But even beyond Doc Beeman's unusual methods, he was known far and wide for "just plain doctorin'" that endeared him to folks.

He didn't mind, for instance, if people with minor ailments would come and sleep on the office porch at night so as to wait for daytime and get the daytime rate.

And even then, if they couldn't pay in cash he accepted vegetables or other farm products instead. Once, a man gave Doc six geese in payment. He put them in his buggy pulled by his sorrel horse, Prince, and started home. By the time he got there, all but one of the geese had flown away. Doc kept the single gander and made a pet of it, naming it Alex. The gander stayed under the porch and would not come out for anyone except Doc Beeman.

Alex outlived his master. When Doc Beeman died in May, 1903, Alex came out from under the porch and forlornly wandered around the cemetery for several days.

Mary Ward, Beeman's great-granddaughter, now lives in the Beeman homeplace and often takes visitors across the road to view the "I Fed Fever" legend engraved on the footstone in the family cemetery. The little graveyard is a quarter of a mile east of Peachland, on the north side of Secondary Road 1416, just west of where it junctions with Secondary Road 1415.

"The little wooden office Dr. Beeman used stood alongside our house there until recent years," Mrs. Ward said. "But it finally got in too bad a shape to keep up even as an outbuilding."

Kegs and Clocks,
a Cabin Step, a Talking Box

It took a lot of work to build a tombstone shaped exactly like a grandfather clock. But it was the perfect symbol for clock repairman Zemri Lamb. Z. N. Lamb died 13 minutes before noon, so his epitaph is told by two hands set at that time on the clockface.

Lamb's tombstone along U. S. Highway 220-B at Level Cross in Randolph County is made of white quartz stones, locally called "white flint," a common rock found in the red Piedmont soil. A small footstone is also built of white flint. Scratched in the concrete cap atop the stone is "1835-1924."

"My uncle George built that tombstone," said Zemri Lamb's grandson, Giles Lamb. "He built it that way because my grandfather was a clock fixer and a cabinet maker."

Another grandson, Corbitt Lamb, vaguely remembers a family story of another sort.

"I think there was some talk that my grandfather had a grandfather clock and that his family couldn't decide who should get it after he died. So, the tale goes, it was settled by taking it to the graveyard where it was used as a form which Uncle George used to shape the stone monument. In other words, the monument is supposed to contain the original clock and the time was set to the minute and hour my grandfather died."

Zemri Lamb got started in clock repairs early in life. "I have a copy of the 1880 census that lists him as a cabinetmaker," said Giles Lamb, "but everyone feels quite sure he was fixing clocks back then too. Back then he was living in the New Salem area, I believe. He had

A grandfather clock stands as the monument to Zemri Lamb. This marker is in Randolph County. Inset is a photograph of Lamb.

a large family, as many as eight or nine children, I recollect. My grandfather, from what I gather, was right much of a practical joker and known for his witty sayings."

A granddaughter, Maggie Hurley, has memories of her grandfather when he lived at Randleman. "Those were his last years, I'd guess. He lived with my aunt at her home on Academy Street. He had a little shop just in back of the house. I think it was torn down when they widened that street and had to move the house back."

Lamb's monument bears no written message, but it is every bit as meaningful as the epitaph of a watchmaker buried in Lidford Churchyard, Devon, England:

Here lies in horizontal position
The outside case of
George Rouleigh. a watchmaker
Whose ability in that line was
An honor to his profession.
Integrity was the main spring.
And Prudence the regulator
Of the actions of his life.
Humane, generous and liberal.
His hand never stopped
Until he had relieved distress.
So nicely regulated were his
Movements that he never
Went wrong
Except when set a-going
By people who did not know
His key.
Even then he was easily
Set right again.
He had the art of disposing
His time so well
That his hours glided
Away in one continual round of
Pleasure and delight, until an
Unlucky moment put a period to

His existence.
He departed this life.
November 14th, 1802.
Age 57.
Wound up in hopes
Of being taken in hand
By His Master and of being
Thoroughly cleaned, repaired
And set a-going in the world
To come.

* * *

BRITISH
Naval Officer
Buried Standing
In Salute
to
His Majesty
King George II

The stark white rectangle with those intriguing words is at Beaufort's Old Burying Ground in Carteret County. Is the military man really buried in a standing position? We can only go by the sign and oral history.

Some say the Royal Navy officer died in 1744, while others allude to the time of the American Revolution, some 30 years later. Some sources say the military man was not an officer at all, but a 19-year-old sailor of ordinary rank. There is also a difference of opinion as to whether he died at sea or while aboard a ship in the port of Beaufort.

But one thing all sources do agree upon. The dying man requested he be buried in uniform standing in salute to the King of England.

There is an old verse that perfectly fits the situation and it is often cited when the Beaufort burial is mentioned:

Resting 'neath a foreign ground,
Here stands a sailor of Mad George's crown.
Name unknown. and all alone,
Standing in the Rebel's ground.

* * *

If you want to read the words on William Jeffreys' tombstone, you will have to climb a ladder. And, you'll have to tote your own to his tomb in Franklin County.

Instead of being buried six feet under, Jeffreys is buried eight feet high. His grave is atop a large boulder that stands on the edge of a wooded area just off U.S. Highway 401 where it junctions with Secondary Road 1001. Only those who scale the gigantic rock or use a ladder get to see the tomb.

A flat marble slab covers a coffin-sized niche that was chiseled in the stone where Jeffreys was entombed. On it are these words:

Attorney at law and Senator
from Franklin
In the General Assembly
Of 1844.

He was a kind husband and parent,
An honest man
And an able and faithful
Public servant.
The fondness of a creature's love,
How strong it strikes the senses!
Thither the warm affection move,
Nor can we call them there.

'Tis finished, 'tis done, the spirit is fled!
The prisoner's gone, the Christian is dead!
The Christian is living through Jesus' love,
And gladly receiving a Kingdom above!

At right, a highway marker on U.S. 401 in Franklin County for the rock tomb of William A. Jeffrey. Below, the actual rock tomb itself.

Although now partially hidden in woods, at one time the boulder in which William Jeffreys is entombed was on the edge of an open field, a prominent landmark at his family's plantation home, Rock Rest. Jeffreys played on the huge, lone boulder as a child, and when he fell critically ill with a fever at age 28, after finishing his first term in the legislature, he expressed a deathbed wish to be entombed in the stone that had given him so much pleasure.

He died October 3, 1845, and his family gave him a temporary burial until a rock mason could chip a slot in the boulder for his eternal rock rest.

* * *

This curious epitaph is to be found at the Old Burying Ground on Ann Street in Beaufort:

Little Girl
Buried
In
Rum Keg.

No one knows her name, but she is not the only person of tidewater Carolina who was laid to rest in a coffin of spirit-soaked wood. In Wilmington, another young woman was also buried in a keg of rum, although her tombstone does not say so. Each died aboard a sailing ship far from land. And in each case, a grieving father chose not to have his daughter buried at sea but returned home preserved in alcohol.

The tale of the Beaufort girl goes back to the early 1800s. The daughter of a shipping merchant, she begged her father to take her on one of his frequent trips to London. Her mother didn't want her to go and withheld permission. But on the girl's 12th birthday, her mother relented on her father's promise that no matter the circumstances he would see that the girl got back home.

All went well during the visit to London, but the girl became ill on the voyage back and died several days later. The ship's crew readied a plank for her burial at sea, but her father prevailed upon the officers to allow him to take his daughter back home as he promised. He purchased a barrel of rum from the ship's hold and sealed her body in it. At Beaufort, the barrel was taken ashore and buried intact.

A gray cross at Wilmington's Oakdale Cemetery marks the grave of Nancy Martin, called Nancé by her family. The family plot in which she is buried tells of a ocean voyage that robbed a ship's captain of his two children.

Shipowner Silas Martin took his daughter, Nancé, and son, John, with him when he set out on an around-the-world cruise from Wilmington in 1857.

Well into the trip, still months from home, Nancé became seriously ill and died on May 25, 1857. She was 24. Her father could not bring himself to throw his beloved daughter's body overboard to the sharks. so he placed it in a barrel of rum and sailed sadly on.

Four months after his daughter's death, Silas Martin's son was washed over the side in stormy seas. Martin kept his vessel in the area for a while, hoping his son's body would be found, but it never was. Not until two months later did he finally arrive back at Wilmington to tell the rest of his family the dreaded news.

It was a solemn procession that followed the flower-bedecked rum barrel to Oakdale Cemetery. Fearing deterioration, Martin had ruled against having his daughter's remains removed and placed in a regular coffin.

Nancé's grave was marked with a cross of stone logs with her nickname on it. The family obelisk that bears her full name and birth and death dates also lists her brother:

John Salter Martin
"Lost At Sea"
Sept 1857
Age 24.

The deaths did not discourage later members of the Martin family from ocean voyages. The tomb of Cuthbert Martin (1875-1922) is engraved:

An unknown child has this epitaph in the Old Burying Ground in Beaufort.

Above, the marker for Nancy 'Nancé' Martin, also buried in a keg of rum. At right, her family marker notes both her death and that of her brother, John. These stones are in Wilmington

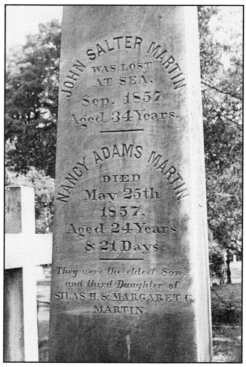

JOHN SALTER MARTIN
WAS LOST AT SEA,
Sep. 1857
Aged 34 Years.

NANCY ADAMS MARTIN
DIED
May 25th
1857,
Aged 24 Years
& 21 Days.

They were the eldest Son
and third Daughter of
SILAS H. & MARGARET C.
MARTIN.

Sunset And Evening Star
And One Clear Call For Me.
And May There Be No Moaning At The Bar
When I Put Out To Sea.

* * *

George Auman is buried under his doorstep. The rock that once offered entrance to his cabin was taken to his grave, stood upright, and used as a tombstone. It is engraved:

This Stone
Was Used
For
Doorstep
By
George Auman.

Auman was born in 1791 and lived his life in a cabin along Little River in the wilderness of the Uwharrie mountains in northern Montgomery County. When he died in 1840, he was buried in a field within sight of his front porch.

Later, the big doorstep suggested itself as a tombstone for his grave, not only because it had been part of his life for lo, so many years, but also because it signified the rugged lifestyle of his times.

Auman's cabin is gone now, but its front step still stands on his grave along a dirt lane just west of Asbury community's ballfield along Secondary Road 1354 off U.S. Highway 220, put there by a great-grandson, Charles Auman. Eventually, the stone and George Auman's remains must be moved, because they are in an area destined to be a four-lane bypass for U.S. 220. Plans are to rebury Auman at Asbury Church Cemetery, several hundred yards east, and to transfer his doorstep as well.

* * *

Some people in Union County have called it "The Talking Tombstone." But that is not an accurate description. True, Uncle Cam

Townsend is buried at the spot and can be heard, loud and clear. But the voice does not come from his handsome headstone. His utterances come from a tape recorder in a weatherproof dias a few feet away.

An engraved plaque tells the visitor:

You are invited to hear excerpts
From a message by
Uncle Cam Townsend
Recorded Dec. 12, 1981
At Biola University.
Press button below
To hear message in
Mr. Townsend's own voice.

William Cameron Townsend was the founder of Wycliffe Bible Translators and its transportation arm, JAARS, the Jungle Aviation and Radio Service. The groups do missionary work, translating the Bible into all the languages of Earth.

Affectionately known as Uncle Cam, Townsend died April 23, 1982, at 86. He was buried alongside the Mexican Museum at the International headquarters of JAARS along Secondary Road 1113, five miles south of Waxhaw in Union County. On his stone is a message for any who may overlook the tape recording:

Dear Ones:

By Love serve one another.
Finish the task.
Translate the Scriptures
Into every language.

Uncle Cam.

Heroes and Heroines

Food was scarce in the war-ravished South in April of 1865.

So Rebecca Alford, of near Holly Springs in Wake County, was delighted to remember she had a hambone. She got it out and started to boil it. April was abloom, so she may have put some wild creecy greens in with it. An advance scouting party of Yankee soldiers got a whiff of the aroma and sought the source. After tracing it to Mrs. Alford's place, they tried to take the dinner pot from her. Rather than give it to them, she sloshed the boiling liquid on them. Howling in pain, the Yankees could think only of medical relief and dashed from the house.

Mrs. Alford was 43 at the time, the mother of seven children. Her tombstone tells how she:

Whipped Sherman's Bummers
With scalding water.

What the Yankees didn't know when they tried to take her pot was that Rebecca Jones Alford had been cooking her hambone to feed a few of her Confederate "soldier boys" who were nearby. What she probably didn't know was that she had faced the point of the entire Union Army.

General William Tecumseh Sherman's army was approaching Raleigh from its devastating march through Georgia, the capture of Savannah, and the burning of Columbia, S.C., and Rebecca Alford's home was in its direct path. Some of Sherman's advance bummers, as they were called, had reached the Alford farm, and they were not

REBECCA JONES
Wife of
G. H. ALFORD
BORN
Mar. 18, 1822,
DIED
Aug. 6, 1890.
Aged 68yrs. 4mos.18ds.
A devoted christian mother who whipped Shermans Bummers with scalding water while trying to take her Dinner Pot which contained a ham bone being cooked for her Soldier Boys.

During the Civil War, General Sherman's men got more than they bargained for when they tangled with Rebecca Jones Alford. Her grave is in Wake County.

used to anyone or anything standing in the way of their demands.

But Rebecca Alford, alone and defiant, was more than they had bargained for. She was the wife of G. H. Alford, a captain of the Home Guards and plantation owner, and two of her sons, George and Andrew, were serving in the Confederate Army, and she was not about to let their enemies be nourished by her hand.

Her stand against Sherman's men made her a heroine to her neighbors. She lived another 25 years after the war and died at 68 in August, 1890. She was buried at Pleasant Grove Baptist Cemetery near the intersection of Secondary Roads 1375 and 1393 north of Fuquay-Varina. Her eldest son, George, who ironically lived in the Leslie House, which had been commandeered as headquarters of Gen. Sherman's North Carolina occupation forces in 1865, decided not to let the legend of his mother die with her. He had her tombstone engraved with these words:

A devoted Christian mother
Who whipped Sherman's bummers
With scalding water
While trying to take her dinner pot
Which contained a ham bone
Being cooked for her
Soldier boys.

Rebecca Alford's house stood until 1975 when it burned to the ground.

* * *

Only a few years after the Civil War, a young black man was buried in a cemetery reserved only for whites four miles south of Coleridge in Randolph County, an act unheard of in those times.

His epitaph at Pleasant Grove Christian Church Cemetery, along Secondary Road 2876 just west of N.C. Highway 22 tells why:

In 1874, Jim Pool saved the lives of William Brown and Levi Cox before dying in the effort. This gravestone is in Randolph County.

JIM POOL, COLORD
Died in 1874
Age 19 Years
Lost his life in saving
the lives of William Brown
and Levi Cox in a well
being dug at William Brown's.

Jim Pool's heroic rescue took place at the home of William Brown about three and a half miles west of the graveyard. Levi Cox, who was 25, and William Brown, 33, had been digging a well at Brown's home. Among those hoisting out the dirt and rock by rope and bucket was Jim Pool.

At an unrecorded depth, the diggers hit a gas pocket and began to gasp for breath. Pool climbed down the well, telling the other rope-pullers to hoist up the incapacitated men when he fastened them to the rope. By the time the rope was lowered the second time Pool himself was gasping for air.

He barely managed to tie the second man securely before he, too, fainted.

Although pulled from the well as rapidly as possible, Pool never recovered from the lethal carbon dioxide in his lungs and died on the lawn nearby. Cox and Brown recovered, and after a few weeks rest, directed the completion of the well.

Meanwhile, Jim Pool had been buried along the edge of the graveyard at Pleasant Grove, a church organized by Thomas C. Moffitt in 1842. Tombstones were an expensive item in the poverty-stricken South of 1874, and none was erected immediately at Pool's grave, but later enough money was raised for one.

William Brown lived another 35 years and died in 1909 at 68. Levi Cox lived 60 more years and died in 1934 at 85. Both are buried about 100 feet from Jim Pool, whose death allowed them long lives.

* * *

The epitaph of William Ellerbrook in Oakdale Cemetery on 15th Street in Wilmington tells a story not only of courage but of faithfulness.

The citizens of Wilmington,
The several fire companies,
And the Christian Association of
St. Paul's Evangelical Lutheran Church
Have erected this monument
To the memory of
Capt. William A. Ellerbrook
A native of Hamburg, Germany
Who lost his life
In doing service at a fire
Corner Front and Dock Streets.
April 11, 1880.

At 24, Ellerbrook was a captain on a Cape Fear River steamboat. When a store on the waterfront caught fire, he happened to be ashore. He dashed inside to help the trapped or injured. As he called out for those inside, his dog Boss heard him and dashed in after him.

The next day searchers found Ellerbrook held fast under a charred ceiling timber that had fallen on him. Boss's remains were by his side, and it appeared the dog had pulled hard on his master's clothes, trying to drag him free.

They were buried in the same casket, and Ellerbrook's tombstone bears a bas-relief carving of a dog and a special line in honor of Boss:

Faithful Unto Death.

* * *

Rose O'Neal Greenhow of Washington, D.C., had no trouble in deciding which side to be on when the Civil War broke out. She had been born below the Mason-Dixon Line, so she felt no qualms about becoming a spy for the Confederacy. She died in line of duty and was buried in Wilmington's Oakdale Cemetery.

Mrs. Rose O'N Greenhow
A Bearer Of Dispatches
To The Confederate Government.
Drowned Off Fort Fisher
From The Steamer Condor
While Attempting To Run
The Blockade.

Rose Greenhow was a teenager when she moved to Washington from her Maryland birthplace in 1830. Attractive, she was invited to many parties and had many suitors. She eventually married a well-known doctor and became a mother of four children. Her husband had a fall one day and died from his injuries. In due and proper time, men began to pay attention to the widow, and she was soon in the social whirl again.

When war broke out in 1861, Rose Greenhow's sympathies were with the southern cause. She found it easy to spy by flirting and listening. She held many parties at her house attended by high-ranking military officers and governmental officials. To each she lent her ear, and they spilled many secrets that went south next morning by courier. Reports she sent to southern leaders were instrumental in several battles, including the defeat of federal forces at Manasses.

But Allen Pinkerton, who was in charge of military intelligence and later was to start the famed Pinkerton Detective Agency, became suspicious of Rose Greenhow. He had her taken into custody under wartime powers and put into prison. But Mrs. Greenhow raised such a fuss over her arrest and caused so much havoc at the prison, including displaying some hastily made Confederate flags from the jail windows, that the federals decided to get rid of her. They sent her across the Virginia border to Richmond.

In Dixie, she was hailed a heroine and sent on a European trip to drum up support for the South. While making a return trip in the fall of 1864, she was aboard a blockade runner called the Condor. Yankee gunboats were near the mouth of the Cape Fear River in North Carolina, where the Condor was headed, and one of them chased the ship, which sailed upstream as quickly as possible. But a partly sunken ship was blocking the channel and the Condor had to swerve. It hit a sandbar.

Rose Greenhow feared being captured by the Yankees and insisted that a rowboat be lowered so she could get to shore. She had a pack of secret documents on her and about $2,000 in gold coins sewed into the hems of her petticoat and dress. Rose and two sailors started for shore, but the boat capsized and Rose, weighted by the gold, plummeted to the bottom. Her body was recovered, and she was given a military funeral with a Confederate flag enclosed in her pine coffin.

Was she a spy? Rose O'Neal Greenhow always said she didn't steal any secrets. The Yankees just volunteered them when she batted her eyes and flashed her smile.

Politicking at the Pearly Gate

A crudely engraved slab of soapstone hidden deep in the woods of North Carolina's Sandhills in Moore County tells the most interesting fact of Marble N. Taylor's life in a single short line:

Gov. N. C. 1 Day.

The Civil War had just begun, and along North Carolina's coast many people were fearful of invasion by Yankee troops. Some were so alarmed that they decided it would be best to make a formal request to rejoin the Union, thus removing themselves from reprisal. They called a "convention," set up a pseudo state government, and elected Marble N. Taylor as "Provisional Governor."

The convention supposedly represented 45 coastal area counties, but only 20 people attended. The session elected not only a governor but named Charles H. Foster as a congressman as well. Foster was never seated, and "Governor" Taylor held office only one day, for the federal government failed to recognize the convention.

A Methodist minister who originally came from Virginia, Marble was scorned not only by his neighbors but by his church for accepting the spurious governorship. According to historian John G. Barrett, "Taylor had been assigned to the Cape Hatteras Mission in December, 1860, by the N.C. Methodist Conference. But one year later he was unceremoniously voted out as a traitor to his conference, his state and the Southern Confederacy."

After the war, Taylor moved to Fayetteville, where he became a successful merchant. Some years later, he began selling fruit trees in the Sandhills. It is believed he married a Moore County woman and settled in Moore for his remaining days.

Moore County surveyor and historian Rassie Wicker has written that Taylor "is said to have been a confirmed atheist and was looked upon by his Calvinistic neighbors with horror. His infidelity forbade Christian rites at his funeral. Long before his death he made an agreement with Bain Frye, a neighborhood fiddler, to play 'Napoleon's Retreat' at his graveside."

Bain Frye died before before Taylor. However, one of Frye's relatives carried out the fiddling assigment, later admitting that he felt uneasy taking part in what he called a "heathen burial."

Not until 125 years after the Civil War did Taylor get a recognizable tombstone on his almost lost grave east of Bensalem in upper Moore County.

In 1985, former county commissioner Anthony "Tony" Parker led a party of hikers to the isolated grave one mile southeast of the firetower at the junction of N.C. Highway 705 and Secondary Road 1270.

"I first visited this site in 1975," Parker said. "Harold Blue and the late Moses Jackson were with me. Moses Jackson had hunted and cut pulpwood all over these parts for a good many years. He was well aware of Taylor's gravesite."

It was in the 1930s that Rassie Wicker first came upon the Taylor grave while surveying south of Robbins. He marked it with pine knots.

"When I found the grave many years later," Parker said. "Wicker's lighter wood pine knots were still there. And you know, after all those years, the ends that Wicker split with an axe to insert little slips of paper markers still had tiny bits of paper left in the cracks. Well, we came back another time after that and brought two small, brown field stones, and we scratched Taylor's name on them."

Those stones were still at the site, but the scratched letters were weathered and difficult to see. A larger, soapstone slab carried in by the 1985 group was erected. On it, crudely engraved was the single line:

M.N. Taylor Gov. N.C. 1 Day.

* * *

The words on William L. Saunders' tombstone were not meant to
be amusing, yet many passersby get a chuckle from them:

I Decline To Answer.

William Saunders' name is familiar to few North Carolinians
now, and some might find it difficult to believe that:

For Twenty Years He
Exerted More Power
In North Carolina
Than Any Other Man.

But his tombstone on the St. James Street side of Calvary Episcopal Church Cemetery in Tarboro lists the sources of his power:

Soldier-Editor-Historian
Statesman And Patriot.
Colonel. 46th Regiment. N.C. Troops.

Distinguished For Wisdom, Purity And His Courage.

A prominent historical marker in downtown Tarboro says that
Saunders, who lived from 1835 to 1891, was even more:

Editor "Colonial Records
Of North Carolina."
Confederate Colonel
N.C Secretary Of State
1879-81.

Two unusual incidents occurred in William Saunders' life, and
both involved his mouth.

During a lull in a Civil War battle, Saunders heard or saw
something that he thought amusing and began laughing out loud. As
he laughed, a bullet passed between his lips and tore a hole in his

At left, the marker for Marble N. Taylor, who was Governor of North Carolina for one day. This marker is in Moore County. Directly below, Abner Sharpe's headstone, located in Iredell County, leaves no doubt as to his political affiliation. At bottom, William Saunders' grave in Tarboro.

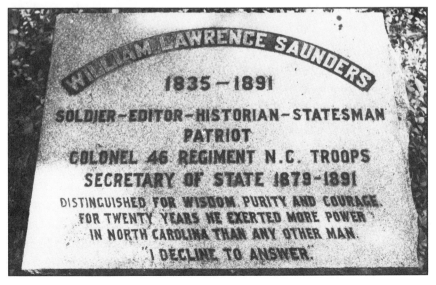

115

cheek. His fellow soldiers remarked it was the most short-lived laugh of the entire war.

A half dozen years after the war, Saunders found it prudent to keep his mouth shut. In April, 1871, Congress passed an "Enforcement Act" which gave federal courts jurisdiction over complaints involving violations of amendments to the Constitution. A congressional group called The Scott Committee investigated violations in the South during Reconstruction.

William Saunders was among the witnesses ordered to appear at one hearing. Some of the committee members had heard reports that he might be an official in the local Klan known as "The Invisible Empire," and held the title of "Emperor." Although threatened with imprisonment for failure to answer the committee's questions, Saunders refused under the Fifth Amendment, replying over and over, "I decline to answer." They became the final words on his tombstone.

* * *

Abner Sharpe wanted everyone to know just where he stood in politics even after he was gone. His tombstone at Oakwood Cemetery in Statesville offers but one proclamation:

HE WAS A DEMOCRAT.

Not much is known about Abner Sharpe. A carpenter, he was born in Iredell County and lived most of his life in Statesville. He died in 1927 at 69.

His obituary in the *Statesville Landmark* said that he worked at odd jobs in his retirement years. In 1926, the year before he died, he was appointed janitor of the courthouse, which could explain the proud proclamation on his tombstone.

* * *

Dr. William C. Wilkings was a refined and cultured man. It says so on the monument erected to his memory at Oakdale Cemetery in Wilmington. So refined was Dr. Wilkings that he fought a duel over politics. He is believed to be the last man in the South to die in a political duel. His monument makes clear his political leanings:

116

Erected By The Members
Of The
Democratic Association
Of The
Town Of Wilmington
For The Memory Of
Dr. Wm. C. Wilkings
One Of Their Late Officers;
And As A Mark Of
Their High Appreciation
Of His Character
As A Citizen, A Friend,
And A Patriot.
Gifted By Nature And Refined
By Cultivation.
Ardent And Generous
In His Impulses.
Eloquent And Fearless In The
Expression Of His Sentiments,
Dr. Wilkings Naturally
Attracted To Himself The Esteem
And Regard Of A Large Circle
Of Admiring Friends
Who Anticipated For Him
A Bright Career Of
Future Usefulness.
That Career Has Been Suddenly Closed
And The Hopes Founded Upon It
Buried With Him In His
Untimely Grave.
But His Memory Survives
And Will Long Be Treasured
In The Hearts Of
His Friends.
May, 1856.

Wilmington's politics were lively in the mid-1850s, and Dr. Wilkings, a Democrat, was actively involved. During a local election campaign, Wilkings assailed the slate of candidates for commissioners of navigation put up by the opposing American, or "Know Nothing" Party. One of those candidates, Joseph H. Flanner, took offense, and his cutting remarks about the Democrats (he called them "Sand Hill Tackies") prompted Wilkings to challenge him to a duel. Flanner offered to settle the matter without violence, but Wilkings said no. Seconds were named, and Flanner, the challenged party, chose weapons: pistols at 10 paces.

Because North Carolina had strong laws against dueling, the group took carriages to Fair Bluff in Columbus County and stepped across the state line into South Carolina. In the first volley, Wilkings grazed Flanner's arm (Flanner later claimed that he shot into the air). Aides tried to settle the affair after that, but neither agreed. Wilkings missed his second shot, but Flanner put his through his opponent's hat. After this round, the seconds almost worked out a settlement, but it broke down over who would make a written apology. In the third volley, Wilkings fell with a bullet in his lung and died within minutes.

The great outcry that followed the senseless death is thought to have brought an end to political dueling in the South.

* * *

"Rest In Peace" might just as well have been lip service as far as Benjamin Smith was concerned. The body of the former North Carolina governor has been dug up twice.

The first time, his creditors dug up his corpse to inform him that he forgot to pay all his debts before he died. It mattered little to them that Governor Smith had donated 20,000 acres of land to the University of North Carolina and had done other good deeds.

These gentlemen in Brunswick County in the early 1800s wanted the money Smith owed them, corpse or not. They held a legal proceeding over his body so they could claim to the courts that they had properly notified Smith, or what was left of him, about his shortcomings.

The second time Smith was dug up, he was treated with more

respect. It was decided that Smith, once a military and public official, should have a more prominent resting place than an unmarked grave in the tiny cemetery at Smithville, a community which later became Southport. So his remains were moved to St. Philips Cemetery at old Brunswick, now Brunswick Town State Historic Site, off N.C. Highway 133 north of Southport.

In 1929, Smith was given a huge marble slab to cover the top of his brick-walled mound. It bears this epitaph:

BENJAMIN SMITH
Soldier And Statesman
1756-1826
Colonel in Revolutionary Army
Governor Of North Carolina
1811
Grand Master Of Masons
1808-1809-1810.

Graciously, nothing is said about him having died in poverty due to his great generosity. At the time of his death, his body was claimed by his creditors as a means of forcing his relatives to pay his debts. But the body was stolen by friends and secretly buried at night to prevent his creditors from levying his body, which was permitted by law at that time. His creditors found the grave anyway and secured a warrant to dig up the body to serve the process on it.

It was an embarassing ending for a once prominent man, especially for a former governor who had been born to wealth and acquired even more on his own. In his time, he owned Blue Banks Plantation and Orton Plantation. He lived at Belvedere Plantation, had homes at Smithville and in Wilmington, and even owned Smith Island, now known as Bald Head Island.

During the Revolutionary War, Smith was an aide-de-camp to General George Washington. In recognition of his service, he was given a grant of 20,000 acres in Tennessee. He gave the land to the University of North Carolina, which named Smith Hall for him.

But Smith was far too magnanimous for his own good. He became surety for a friend. The friend's dealings fell through, and Smith was responsible for huge debts. He began to mortgage his holdings and eventually lost everything. He died a pauper on January 10, 1826.

Few people today know that he fought two duels and was wounded in one. He recovered but carried the bullet to his grave. Years later, when Smith's remains were to be moved to a more prominent site on state land, that bullet served to identify him.

According to one report, the woman who held the lantern at Smith's first, secret burial was still living in the area. She was contacted and agreed to show authorities which was Smith's grave. After the grave was reopened, the old woman got down in it, sifted through the soft dirt, bones and other debris and finally found what she was looking for. She held up a bullet and said, "This is the bullet that wounded General Smith during one of his duels. This is the right grave."

Feathers, Fur, and Fins

When Lockhart Gaddy fell dead in 1963, the wild geese he was feeding at his pond went silent. Called "Father Goose" by many of his friends, Gaddy was buried on the shore of his beloved Anson County lake, which was known across the nation as "Gaddy's Goose Pond." The top of his tombstone is engraved:

God Is Our Refuge.
— Psalm 46.

Gaddy and his wife Hazel operated a refuge for migrating waterfowl unlike any other that ever existed. After Gaddy's death, his wife kept the refuge going until she died in 1972. Their double tombstone is surrounded by a granite border which is engraved:

Friends Of Wildlife.

Ironically, Lockhart Gaddy had started out an avid goose hunter. In 1926, he bought five wild geese, clipped their wings, and used them as decoys each winter to attract geese that migrated from Canada to North Carolina. When live decoys were outlawed, Gaddy kept his geese as pets on his farm east of N.C. Highway 52 in Anson County.

In the early 1930s, Gaddy built a one-acre fish pond, mostly for the angling pleasure of his 80-year-old mother-in-law, Pattie Ross. Even though the pond was a mile from Gaddy's home, his pet geese found their way there and made it their second home. In the winter of

1934, these one-time decoys enticed nine of their wild relatives to settle on the pond. Gaddy was so surprised and pleased that he gave up his gun forever for the new-found pleasure of bird watching.

The following winter, the wild geese returned, bringing five additional geese. Within five years, at least 100 wild geese were returning to the pond each winter from Canada for the free corn and safe haven Gaddy was offering. Not only did Gaddy raise grain to keep the geese coming, he enlarged his pond to four acres to offer more spacious accommodations.

By 1952, an estimated 10,000 Canada geese were wintering at Gaddy's Goose Pond, as the refuge had come to be called. Another thousand ducks and geese of other varieties came as well. People came in even greater numbers. Mrs. Gaddy said that in the winter of 1952-53, visitors came from 47 states and 11 foreign countries to see the geese. She counted 29,679 names in the guest register for that season alone.

Among the visitors were wildlife experts who marveled that anyone could get within arm's reach of the usually wary geese. But Lockhart and Hazel Gaddy could. Geese that would have nothing to do with humans off the refuge would take bread from their hands.

Lockhart Gaddy was feeding his geese when he suddenly toppled over and died. His wife, who was at his side, reported the geese became silent for a long moment. There was only one appropriate place for Gaddy to be buried. He was laid to rest alongside his pond. When the preacher asked for a prayer at his funeral, silence prevailed not only among the humans but among the geese as well. Few even moved. When the funeral was over and all visitors had gone except close relatives, the geese came to Gaddy's grave, as if paying their last respects.

By the time Hazel Gaddy was buried alongside her husband in 1972, the United States Government had bought land nearby and created the Pee Dee National Wildlife refuge. But the Gaddy acreage and pond remained in private hands. Tom Pond, a great-nephew, owns it now.

"The pond itself is quite grown up," he said while leading a visitor to the small lake on a private road off Secondary Road 1635. "It is rimmed with trees and lots of bushes are around it. Not many geese

On Willie Brower's tombstone in Chatham County is carved a likeness of his favorite dog, Prince.

James Earl 'Mose' Kidd is buried in Moore County, where he enjoyed 'coon hunting.

Clarence Don Barber's nickname was 'Buckshot.'
This grave is in Guilford County.

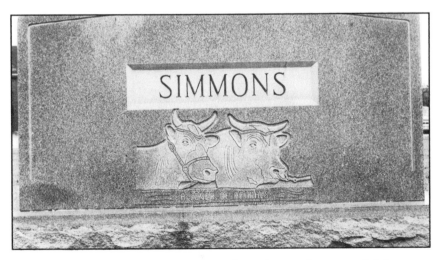

The heads of two cows are engraved on the tombstone of dairy
farmer Mrs. Emma Simmons, located in Chatham County.

come anymore because conditions have changed. No one is keeping the lake cleared, and no one is feeding the geese as my great aunt and uncle used to do. Anyway, the goverment has thousands of acres of wildlife refuge along the Pee Dee River, and I suppose that takes the place of what used to go on here."

A weathered old building sits along the shoreline. Once it had been a concession stand where visitors could buy small sacks of corn to feed the geese. The lonely graves of James Lockhart and Hazel Ross Gaddy have been surrounded by trees, and squirrels are more likely to scamper over their graves now than waddling fowl. But in the gray of winter, the high, honking of geese flying overhead is still heard.

* * *

A troublesome bird dog decorates the tombstone of Willie Brower, a retired farmer, dog trainer, and hunting lodge operator, who died at 80 in 1981 and was buried at Brush Creek Cemetery at the junction of Secondary Roads 1100 and 1129 in southeastern Chatham County.

"That is a picture of Prince on Daddy's tombstone," said his son, William.

"At one time the late Judge Moody owned Prince but couldn't control him. He brought the young dog to Daddy and said Prince had just about bitten everyone in Siler City at some time or another. He told Daddy if he could do something with the dog, he could have him. Daddy told Judge Moody to put the dog in the barn. The two men then walked back to the judge's car. Daddy thanked him and the judge drove off.

"Daddy went to the barn and opened the door, but Prince growled, bared his teeth, and wouldn't let Daddy in. Daddy wasn't going to let any dog keep him out of his own barn. He grabbed Prince up by the skin of the neck, snatched him over his head and flung him to the far end of the barn. Daddy glared at the dog, daring it to make a false move. Prince slowly crawled on his belly to Daddy and licked his hand. That is the story I heard more than once from my father."

From that day on, Prince and Willie Brower were almost inseparable companions.

"Then, one day while in Alabama in relation to a dog event, Daddy was offered $500 for Prince," his son said. "You must remember, it was the 1930s and $500 was an awful lot of money. Daddy sold Prince and came back home. There is a story Momma often told us about how daddy didn't eat or sleep very well for weeks on end. One day he said he was going to Alabama. He didn't say why, but when he came back, he had Prince with him and a big smile was on his face. Daddy never did say how much he paid to get Prince back...and you can bet nobody asked him."

Prince lived out his days with Brower, and years later, when Brower fell seriously ill and was facing death, he was still thinking of the dog he had cherished above all others.

"He asked me to see to it that a picture of Prince was carved on his tombstone," his son said. "I agreed. When the time came, I got some pictures we still had of Prince and took them to an Asheboro tombstone carver. The result is what is on daddy's stone."

* * *

Carl Craven, 75 years old, was passing time at a service station on Secondary Road 1003 in Randolph County when a visitor inquired if anybody knew why a rooster decorated the tombstone of Robert F. Bray in a graveyard across the road at Pleasant Ridge Church.

Bray had been born in 1877 and died in 1912, but Craven knew about him, right down to his nickname.

"Bunk Bray used to be very interested in rooster fighting," he said. "He raised some of those fighting cocks, and he'd sure get interested if you mentioned having one that might be able to whip his. Come to think of it, his cousin is down the road just a short distance, building a house. Go down there and ask him. He knows all about it."

The sound of a hammer signaled the house where Fred Bray was working.

"Of course I remember why Bunk has a rooster on his headstone," he said. "Bunk wanted that rooster there, that's why. He ran a grocery store near here and was always interested in knowing if people coming in had any fighting roosters. He'd be tickled to find out you had one and would let it fight one of his.

"He raised some fighting roosters. He had some around all the time. Proud of them, that man was. Rooster fighting went on in those days without much fuss from the law. Bunk had his share of fun out of it, all right. That was his sport. He always did say he wanted a rooster put on his tombstone when he died, and that's what his folks did. They put one there."

Back at the service station, Carl Craven brightened upon learning that his story had been confirmed.

"I'll tell you something else about those stones over there. Did you see the one of Henry Pope's, with a sheep and a dog on it? Henry Pope had been an Arizona sheep rancher. Stayed out there most of his life. When he got older he decided to come back home to finish his days out, I guess. Anyway, this was his home territory, and he wanted to be buried here.

"Henry always wore a long beard. Told me one time he shaved only once in his life. Said that after his first shave he decided that was the last time.

"Henry said he'd like a sheep on his tombstone. Guess they took him at his word. There is a sheep on the stone, and that's fitting for an Arizona sheep rancher, don't you think?"

* * *

Deer and a game fish are emblazoned on the bronze plaque that marks the grave of James Chad Allen at Randolph Memorial Park in north Asheboro. Allen, was killed in an automobile accident while on his way fishing on April 6, 1986. He was 17.

A eulogy in the local newspaper on the first anniversary of his death made clear his love of the outdoors:

> *Fishing and hunting*
> *were his life and sport—*
> *sitting at a pond or in the woods,*
> *not a basketball court.*

The plaque at Allen's grave offers this:

127

I'm but off to more adventure
Knowing still your love and loving you.

* * *

Strangers who pass his tombstone learn that Clarence Don Barber had a popular nickname: Buckshot. It appears in parentheses on his headstone at the Springfield Baptist Church Cemetery in Whitsett in Guilford County.

The nickname is explained by an engraving on the stone: a picture of an antlered deer. A brickmason who was killed at 51 in an accident on an all-terrain vehicle, Barber was a member of The Hunt Club of Whitsett.

* * *

James Earl "Mose" Kidd died in September just as his favorite season approached. Soon crisp, moonlit nights would have lured Kidd into the woods in quest of his favorite quarry: the black-masked, ring-tailed raccoon. Hearing the howling 'coon dogs racing through the night and baying when they treed a 'coon was music to Mose Kidd's ears.

Such nights came to an end in 1982, when Kidd was hurt in a motorcycle accident.

"He suffered a broken leg but wanted to be treated as an outpatient rather than stay in a hospital," said his brother Larry. "A blood clot must have developed and taken his life." Mose Kidd, who had been a water plant employee at Asheboro, was buried at Union Grove Church Cemetery along N.C. Highway 705 in Moore County.

His tombstone pictures a dog baying up a tree at a 'coon, with another raccoon looking on nearby.

* * *

Some people call it a pig, but the animal carved on the flat slab covering Thomas Pollock's grave is really a boar. Pollock is buried in St. Paul's Church Cemetery at Edenton in Chowan County. On two occasions in the early 1700s, he served as the acting governor of the Carolina colony.

The boar symbol was part of the Pollock family crest, which also contained the words, "Strong and Stout." Pollock's Scottish ancestors were given the emblem because an early Pollock saved the life of King James IV from an attack by a wild boar.

* * *

Why are two squirrels pictured on the tombstone of J. L. Henry and two fish engraved on the headstone of his wife?

The couple is buried at Brower's Chapel Church Cemetery along Secondary Roads 2824 and 2826 east of Asheboro in Randolph County. Henry was born in 1859. He died in 1920. His wife was born in 1862. There is no death date upon her stone. Area residents say that Henry liked to squirrel hunt and his wife liked to fish, reason enough for the figures on their tombstones.

* * *

William Bryan Barker found fascination in horses. On his flat grave marker in the central section of the Hebrew Cemetery on High Point Road in Greensboro are these rhymed lines:

He Loved
All God's creatures
Great and small
But a horse
Most of all.

According to a news report at the time of his death, Barker was 24 when he fell off a cliff and was fatally injured while horseback riding in Alexander County on the afternoon of March 17, 1984. The accident happened on Rock Ridge in a mountainous area northeast of Taylorsville. Officials said Barker had dismounted to look over a cliff and apparently slipped and fell about 100 feet, suffering neck and head injuries.

* * *

The heads of two cows are engraved on the tombstone of Mrs. Emma Simmons, a well-known dairy farmer in Chatham County, who died in 1951. She is buried at Pittsboro United Methodist Church Cemetery. Her epitaph may best state the reason that the tombstones of so many North Carolinians are decorated as they are:

A Lover Of Animals.

'Til Death Do Us Part

The marker on the grave of Julia Doris Hines at Bear Branch Cemetery off Secondary Road 1443 near Ledbetter in northern Richmond County is as pink as the rosy peach blossoms waving across hundreds of acres of Sandhills orchards in springtime. The color is significant, for Julia Hines' epitaph calls her:

The Best Peach In The Basket.

Julia Hines died at 23, just before Christmas, 1944, leaving a small child. Her headstone identifies her as the wife of W. Pietrzak, who called her:

My Dossie.

"Yes, there was a love story," said Joe Hines, Julia Hines' younger brother, who operates a business near Hamlet.

As a teenager, Julia was a vivacious, slim brunette whom everyone liked. During and after high school she worked in the local dime store. When World War II was imminent, the Hines family moved to Norfolk, Va., where the adult members got jobs in defense industries. There Julia met a Marine named Walter Pietrzak, whom her family called Pete.

"I'm not sure what year they were married, but Julia and Pete eventually had a child, Walter Jr., a nice red-headed boy," said Joe Hines. "Then the war really got underway, and Pete was sent overseas."

"MY DOSSIE"

JULIA DORIS HINES
WIFE OF
W. PIETRZAK
AUG. 7, 1921
DEC. 18, 1944

"THE BEST PEACH
IN THE BASKET"

The marker on the grave of Julia Doris Hines Pietrzak, in
Richmond County, is pink, like peach blossoms.

Pete, it turned out, would survive the war, but his wife Julia would die at home while he was away.

"My sister got pretty sick, which no one was expecting, because she had gotten a physical examination a few weeks earlier," said Joe. "She passed out and was taken to a military hospital where she made temporary recovery. But overnight she seemed to get worse, and when she woke up and saw a pitcher of orange juice, she asked for and was served some. She had a relapse and never recovered. She died from complications of sugar diabetes. It just wasn't diagnosed, as well as I understand it."

It was a sad Christmas season for the Hines family. And for Walter Pietrzak the heartbreak was even more agonizing. He was overseas and unable to get home for the funeral.

"It couldn't be postponed," Joe said. "Julia was buried the day her son was one year old. When Pete did get home a couple of weeks later, he immediately went to get a headstone. I went with him. I don't know where he got the 'Best Peach' saying he put on the stone. We had never lived on a peach farm, and as far as I know, Julia had never worked in a peach orchard. I don't know that it was original with him. I just don't know. I didn't think it unusual at the time, I guess, because I was so young. I do think it's a nice saying, though.

"One other thing about that stone. Pete had my sister's maiden name put on there because he said everybody knew her by that name and hardly anybody in North Carolina knew him."

Walter Pietrzak returned to the military. His baby son was taken care of for a short while by relatives.

"Pete didn't have any relatives in North Carolina, so he never came here to live. He continued in the service, later remarried, stayed in the military for 20 years until retirement, and then, I believe, settled in California," Joe said. "I do know that is where the child, Walter Jr., grew up and probably is right now, because my brother Harold attended his wedding about 10 years ago."

* * *

"Until death do us part" is a wedding vow that many couples honor even beyond life. Love throughout eternity is expressed on tombstones all across North Carolina.

Great Loves Live On.

So says one tombstone in the cemetery behind the Montgomery County Courthouse in Troy. Those words exemplify the affection that Mattie Jackson (1897-1978) must have felt for her beloved husband, Jesse Shaw, (1893-1948) for they are carved on his tombstone.

* * *

James Bonner loved his wife Sarah so much that when she died at 23 in 1779, he had long, loving, and expensive lines of adoration carved upon her stone at St. Peter's Episcopal Church Cemetery at Washington in Beaufort County:

> *Here lies my wife,*
> *Oh lovely once, and fair;*
> *Her face cast in the*
> *Mould of beauty where*
> *Her eyes all radiance*
> *Her cheeks like snow.*
> *Whose cheeks once tinctured*
> *A purple glow.*
> *Where's those ivory teeth*
> *And lips of celestial sound?*
> *Her lips like lilies*
> *Set with roses 'round?*
> *Where's that soft marble breast,*
> *White neck and where*
> *That all of woman*
> *Past description fair?*
> *Where's those active fingers*
> *That with artful ease*
> *Which in her house once*
> *Taught her family to please?*
> *Where's that sprightly wit,*

Even love's divine delight?
All sunk, alas.
In everlasting night.
Earth take her bones.
Chaste soul she smiles at rest
Whilst her image lives
Immortal in my breast.

* * *

A few of the tombstones at Organ Lutheran Church Cemetery along Secondary Road 1006 in Rowan County are engraved in German. Among the lines on one stone are:

Hier Rufth Mein Mann.

That is one woman's heartfelt way of saying:

Here Lies My Man.

* * *

G. Glossom of Liberty in Randolph County dearly loved his 21-year-old wife, and it tore his heart to lose her after so short a marriage. As his dear Carrie (1867-1888) was laid to rest in the old cemetery at Liberty Grove Methodist Church along Secondary Road 2417, he thought of the great loss, but it also came to him that he should be grateful for having met, married, and shared her love, no matter the brief time. So he had these words carved on her stone:

Lord, she was Thine
And not my own.
Thou has done me no wrong.
I thank Thee for the precious loan
Afforded me so long.

* * *

135

When R. L. Martin's wife, Sallie J., died, he had her interred in The Old Burying Ground at Beaufort in Carteret County. To him, she was spunky, a spirited woman who knew how to take care of herself in every situation.

When it was time for Martin to join her in 1880, he still held his mate in such high esteem that he wanted everyone to know he was proud to be with her for eternity:

Life's fitful fever over.
He sleeps well.
Beside his little hero.

* * *

Nannie B. Hilliard (1887-1972) expressed similar sentiments on her tombstone in the town cemetery behind the courthouse at Troy in Montgomery County:

She Sleepth Beside
The One She Loved.

* * *

The tombstone of James M. Chandler (1869-1930) and Addie R. Varner (1887-1928) at the United Methodist Church Cemetery at New Hope in Randolph County lets all know that they, too, sleep happily and eternally together.

Let no hopeless tears be shed,
Holy is this narrow bed.

* * *

Helen Blair Tredwell has two tombstone in Hayes Cemetery at Edenton in Chowan County. The graveyard is across Queen Anne's Creek, a short distance from the historic Barker House and visitor's center on Edenton's waterfront.

Researcher Linda Jordan Eure discovered the two tombstones while doing a cemetery census as site manager at the James Iredell House in Edenton. The first stone is engraved:

In
Memory of
Helen.
Wife of Samuel Tredwell
Who departed this life
The 24th of February 1802
Aged 29 years and 2 days.

The second says:

To the memory
Of
Helen Blair
Daughter of
George and Jane Blair
And
First wife of
Samuel Tredwell, Esquire.
Born 22nd February 1763
Died 24th February 1802

With a warm heart
And a brilliant intellect
She was universally
Beloved and admired.

According to a brief research note made by Linda Eure, the stone with the shortest inscription apparently was first, for the second mentions that Helen Blair was "the first wife" of Samuel Tredwell.

"It must have been placed there after his marriage to Frances Pollock Lenox," Eure noted. "The second stone is connected to that of Samuel Tredwell on one side and on the other side is the tombstone for Frances Pollock Lenox."

Speculation is that Tredwell's conscience may have bothered him after taking a second wife, prompting him to erect a second stone to his first wife with a more glowing tribute.

* * *

Part of Sarah Pollock's epitaph has been censored, several lines crudely chiseled from the flat slab of stone covering her grave in St. Paul's Episcopal Church Cemetery at Edenton.

The faint epitaph begins with passages of praise for Sarah's loving personality, beautiful face and attractive figure.

So what was chiseled off and why?

Sarah Pollock was the wife of Major George Pollock of colonial days. During the early 1700's, the Pollocks were important people in coastal Carolina. So when Sarah died, her husband arranged for an impressive marble slab to cover her grave. He wanted an epitaph that would do justice to his beloved spouse.

According to legend, Pollock commissioned a local stonecutter to do the job and told him to create a fitting epitaph, giving him freedom to choose the words, so long as they told what a warm and wonderful woman Sarah had been. The result was something more than Pollock had expected. When he went to see the finished stone on his wife's grave and began to read the flowery passages, he immediately realized that the stonecutter knew things about his wife that only he should have known.

Enraged, he went home, got a hammer and chisel, and returned to chip out the most intimate passages. What he did to the stonecutter is not recorded.

* * *

Dear, should anything happen to me, don't
you worry. Don't forget to live a Christian life.
I'll be waiting at the Pearly Gates just as
anxious as the day I met you at the altar.
Goodbye dear,

Signed, Elva.

Those very personal words are on public view on the tombstone of Elva Cox Campbell at Salisbury's Chestnut Hill Cemetery in Rowan County. According to a brief item published by Burlington author Alonzo C. Hall in 1961, the message was written as a suicide note, and Mrs. Campbell's husband chose to use it as an epitaph. However, neither her obituary nor her death certificate indicates that was the case.

Mrs. Campbell died March 15, 1935. She was 53. Her death certificate lists "principal cause of death" as "cerebral hemorrhage" and further mentions a "contributing cause of arteriosclerosis." Her obituary in the *Salisbury Post* states: "Elva Campbell, 52, wife of Henry M. Campbell, well-known fireman for the Southern Railway at Spencer, died early Friday at her home from a sudden heart attack. She was in apparent good health Thursday and was found in an unconscious condition at her home shortly after midnight. She lived some five hours afterward.

"She was a native of Randolph County, a daughter of the late Mr. and Mrs. Timothy Cox. She was married in 1910 and the couple came to Spencer in 1918. She was an honored member of The Sons and Daughters of Liberty at Spencer, she held membership in Washington Counsel and the Spencer Methodist Church. She was an estimable character, loved by all who knew her."

Her grave is just to the left inside the Chestnut Hill Cemetery entrance on U.S Highway 29-70, where a large headstone marks the Campbell plot and three headstones are aligned:

Elva Cox	*Henry*	*Kate Kaddell*
Wife of H.M.	*Mansfield*	*Wife of H.M.*
Campbell	*Campbell*	*Campbell*
1881-1935.	*1886-1966.*	*1888-1959.*

* * *

139

Another grave marker at Salisbury's Chestnut Hill Cemetery not only speaks of love but makes death sound like nothing more than a good night's sleep.

GOOD-NIGHT HONEY.
SEE YOU IN THE
MORNING

James W. Oddie
1904-1953.

The gravestone of James W. Oddie in Rowan County indicates that death is just a good night's sleep.

Kith and Kin

This startling statement is reported to be part of Saint Ethelreda's epitaph in England:

Twice a widow,
Yet always a virgin.

So says *The Book of Days* by Elizabeth and Gerald Donaldson, A&W Publishers, N.Y.,1979. Equally as startling is this "epitaph," which at least one Tar Heel publication claimed to be on a tombstone at Snow Camp in southwestern Alamance County:

Here Lies A Virgin
With A Babe In Her Arms.

Sorry, but there is no such epitaph at Snow Camp, according to local historians and a graveyard census. There is, however, a headstone upon which is carved:

Amy Catherine Stuart
With Sarah Deidama
In Her Arms.

Possibly someone took liberty with the wording on this tombstone, which is located in the oldest section of the burial ground at Cane Creek Friends Meeting. The cemetery is at the junction of Secondary Roads 1005 and 2371. Amy Stuart's resting place is Row 5, Grave 46.

Born May 23, 1851, she died April 2, 1873, at 21.

Despite the lack of "Mrs." or "Consort of," preceeding her name, she was the first wife of David Stuart and had at least two children. A marker alongside her grave shows that she had another daughter, Mary Eleanor, just 18 months before she died in childbirth with Sarah Deidama. Mary Eleanor lived only 18 days.

David Stuart is buried in another row nearby with his second wife.

* * *

Electa S. Smith's gravestone has an unusual variation in the way dates of birth and death are usually carved on tombstones:

On earth June 2, 1889
In Heaven Dec. 22, 1984.

She is buried in Gum Orchard Church cemetery at Zephyr in Surry County. Her epitaph:

When God gave us mothers,
He gave us all love.

* * *

Mothers are known for affection and there can be no doubt what was in the heart of Ethel Allen Staley, who died in 1986 at 96.

Her stone in the city cemetery at Troy in Montgomery County spells it out:

Mama loved Sam, Baby & Kitty.

* * *

Mary Tilson Edwards King, also buried at the city cemetery in Troy, was 61 in 1981, when she was laid to rest with maternal honors. Bold letters on her tombstone declare that she was more than an ordinary mama:

Hannah Hadley is buried at Snow Camp in Alamance County.

Mother Of Men.

The names of her sons follow: Robert Edwards, Isaac Fletcher, Stephen Ernest, Spurgeon Caldwell, Andrew Auman, and Hilary James.

* * *

Hannah Hadley is buried at Snow Camp in Alamance County. She was 74 when she died at the end of the Revolutionary War in 1783. For many years a crude stone marked her grave, but in 1974 a new marker was erected that did justice to her life:

PIONEER MOTHER.

The inscription is illustrated by a figure of a woman in a floor-length dress with a shawl about her shoulders and a sunbonnet atop her head.

* * *

Alexander Allen died in 1835 at 53. His tombstone at Hawfields Presbyterian Church along N.C. Highway 119 southeast of Haw River in Alamance County bears this touching request from his children:

Tread Softly O' er This
Sacred Spot
Beneath, Lies One Yet
Not forgot.
It Is Our Father.

* * *

The tombstone of Samuel L. Little in the churchyard at Reeds Crossroads along N.C. Highway 150 in Davidson County doesn't give a clue as to how many children he left behind when he died in 1983 at the age of 66. But his epitaph shows that they held him in high esteem:

A father is someone you look up to
No matter how tall you grow.

* * *

Tennent I. Bowen was a native of Maryland who came to live in Washington, N. C., and died there in 1812 at 27. A young father, he was buried at First Presbyterian Church Cemetery with this epitaph:

Our friend and father, he is dead
The cold and lifeless clay
Has made in dust its silent bed
And there it must decay.

* * *

Robert Overcash was only 30 when he died and was buried at Organ Lutheran Church along Secondary Road 1006 in Rowan County. His wife and children wanted all to know the enormity of their loss:

This grave holds
All that is near and dear
To wife and five little ones.

* * *

James Cresswell's family wanted to make sure that his generosity was not forgotten. So they left a reminder, right to the penny, on his tombstone at Buffalo Presbyterian Church off 16th Street in Greensboro:

146

In Memory
James Cresswell
Who Died A.D. 1822
In the 76th Year of His Age
Leaving 100 Dollars
To The
N. Buffalo Church.

* * *

Although his gravestone lists him only as "Father," Angus Kelly must have been equally as proud of being a grandfather, for when he died in 1934 at 66, he left a reminder in his epitaph at Bethesda Cemetery on N.C. Highway 5 near Aberdeen in Moore County that grandchildren shouldn't be overlooked:

A Good Man
Leaves An Inheritance
To His Children's
Children.

* * *

This could be North Carolina's most intriguing epitaph:

Pa, don't hold me back!
It is all tangled up
And I can't undo it.

Those words are on the tombstone of Hattie Frizzie, five years old, buried at St. Peter's Episcopal Church Cemetery at Washington in Beaufort County. Hattie died October 16, 1881.

"Pa" was W. Scott Frizzie, but why his daughter begged him not to hold her back is not known. Hattie's mother, Ella J. Frizzie, is also named on her tombstone, a small obelisk on the second row from the cemetery's east wall.

* * *

Two babes were laid in earth
Before she died.
A third now slumbers
At the mother's side.

Those are the somber words on the single stone at Old Smithfield Burying Ground at Southport in Brunswick that identifies the daughters of M.C.S. Anna Crapox simply as "Mary, Carrie and Eva."

* * *

Heaven retaineth now our treasure,
Earth the lovely casket keeps;
And the sunbeams love to linger
Where our little Annie sleeps.

Ann Patterson "sleeps" in Bethesda Cemetery along N.C. Highway 5 at Aberdeen in Moore County. The daughter of D.S. and Kate B. Blue, "Annie" was 14 when she died.

* * *

Bethesda Cemetery also holds the body of 5-year-old Johnnie Malcolm, son of Charles E. and P. B. Pleasants:

No kisses drop upon thy cheek.
Those lips are sealed to me.
Dear Lord, how could I give him up
To any but to Thee?

* * *

Archie Bailey lived less than 90 days. He came into the world on April 26, 1915, and departed July 15. His parents, J. C. and G. E. Bailey, laid their infant in the ground at Center Methodist Church in the Blaine community at the intersection of Secondary Road 1300 and N.C. Highway 109 in Montgomery County.

148

Archie's small, diamond-shaped stone sits on one point and catches the eye not only geometrically but with verse:

The little crib is empty now,
The little clothes laid by;
A mother's hope, a father's joy
In death's cold arm doth lie.
Go little pilgrim, to thy home,
On yonder blissful shore,
We will miss thee here, but soon will come
Where thou hast gone before.

* * *

A teddy bear and building blocks are the kind of toys usually found under a Christmas tree. At Midway Church Cemetery, along Secondary Road 2122 near Randleman in Randolph County, poignant pictures of these playthings are carved in stone at the grave of 5-month-old Kenneth R. Routh, who died on Christmas Day in 1960.

* * *

Lambs are perhaps the most frequently carved symbols seen on the tombstones of infants. One adorns the grave of Charles R. Lambe Jr. at Midway Church Cemetery on Worthville Road in Randolph County. The birth and death dates tell a story:

July 7, 1970
July 7, 1970.

* * *

There are no dates on the tiny marker at Reeds Baptist Church Cemetery along N.C. Highway 150 in Davidson County, only the name of Oscar, the two-year-old son of P.D. and A.R. Finch.

Much of the small marble headstone is blackened with age, but a close examination reveals touching words:

149

We had a little treasure once,
He was our joy and pride.
We loved him Ah! perhaps too well,
For soon he slept and died.

* * *

Elizabeth Garner was 33 when she was buried in 1875 at Lassiter's Mill Cemetery along Secondary Road 1175 in southwestern Randolph County. Her epitaph brings visons of springtime in the Uwharrie Mountains that loom on the skyline beyond her tomb:

Weep not parents, sisters, brothers
She is gone before.

Lizzie is an angel now
Why weep for her today?
Up yonder where there is no death
You can be with her always.

Let flowers bloom about her grave
For she loved them.

* * *

Susan Phillips was only eight when she was buried at Cedar Grove Cemetery in New Bern in 1880:

In Cedar Grove, under a little mound
A flower is planted to bloom on richer ground
Thus flowers from earth by death are driven
To bloom more pure and chaste in heaven
Tears will moisten this lonely sod
Sunshine comes alone from God.

* * *

Marked only as the "Kivett Infant," the small tombstone at Science Hill Friends Cemetery along Secondary Road 1107 in Randolph County speaks also of a flower:

An angel visited the green earth
And took away a little flower.

Feb. 11, 1970-Feb. 11, 1970.

* * *

The verse on John V. White's tombstone at Providence Friends Cemetery northwest of Randleman in Randolph County declares:

I die, but as the springbird dies,
In summer's golden glow to rise.
These were my days of April bloom
My summer is beyond the tomb.

* * *

Evelyn Manson was eight weeks old when her body was carried to The Old Burying Ground at Beaufort in Carteret County:

A sweet little flower
Too tender to stay,
From this world's blast
Was hurried away.

JOSEPH PAUL
DUNLAP
APR. 8, 1910
JAN. 4, 1982

Paul Dunlap nearly made it to the Major Leagues before fighting in World War II. His tombstone, located in Chatham County, shows a right-handed batter. But a former teammate says that Dunlap was a lefty.

The Game of Life

War kept Paul Dunlap from becoming a major league baseball star. Born in Chatham County in 1910, Dunlap grew up playing baseball in the countryside south of Siler City in Chatham County. In high school, he played first base and kept the position when he went on to become a star at the University of North Carolina at Chapel Hill.

After college, he signed with Asheville in the Piedmont League, moved to the outfield, and hit .330 his first year. He soon was spotted by scouts for the New York Yankees, who drafted him and farmed him to Norfolk, where an injury kept him from playing much. The next season he was shifted to Binghamton in the New York-Pennsylvania League, where he hit .375. From Binghamton, he went to Indianapolis.

A newspaper clipping from that year says: "Dunlap has been hitting the ball at a terrific clip all season and at present is not far from the .400 mark. The walloper has the distinction of leading all leagues in organized baseball and has been the topic of conversation throughout the country since he joined the Skiffmen shortly after the 1936 season began."

Other clippings from an old scrapbook tell of periods when Dunlap was batting as high as .500.

Big league baseball seemed to be within Dunlap's grasp, but war was brewing in Europe, and Dunlap went off to the Navy, where he became a Chief Petty Officer and only occasionally saw a baseball diamond. He was 36 when he got discharged after the war, too old, he was told, for big league baseball. He lived out his life in Siler City playing local ball, managing clubs, and umpiring.

"His little mobile home had a quite a few baseball souvenirs in it," recalled his nephew, Ray Dunlap of Garner. "I remember an autographed picture on the wall of Babe Ruth pointing to the spot in the outfield where Ruth planned to hit a homerun. I don't know what happened to that photograph. I wish I had it. I do have one of Uncle Paul's Louisville Slugger bats with his name embossed on it. And I do have this scrapbook that my father kept. I have always wondered too, if there was a baseball card with Paul Dunlap's picture on it.''

Declining health finally forced Dunlap into a medical facility, and after two years of illness, he died at a military hospital at Hampton, Va., on January 4, 1982, just shy of his 72nd birthday. He was buried at Loves Creek Church along Highway 64 in Siler City. A baseball player in uniform, bat poised, is pictured on his tombstone. But a sharp-eyed ballplaying rival of Dunlap's, rest home resident Robert "Crip" Dixon, is quick to point out, "Paul was a left-hand batter. The picture on his stone shows a right-hand batter. It kinda bothered me when I saw that."

* * *

James O. Grimsley, an Asheboro lawyer, was only 32 when he collapsed and died during a run on the track at Asheboro Junior High School on June 2, 1977. A baseball and basketball player in high school, Grimsley had remained a strong athlete and loved all sports.

After he was buried at Oaklawn Cemetery in Asheboro, a tombstone was erected at his grave showing a basketball, tennis racket, golf clubs, and a baseball in the pocket of a glove. His epitaph:

He was as pleasant as a new dawning,
Clean cut as a morning rain.
Good as the rich earth
Producing good fruits.
But now there is a void—
Where once a flower stood.
Stalwart, admired.
Cut down with one clean stroke.

154

Yet who are we to question,
The kind, loving Gardener
Who chose for His bouquet
The very best.

* * *

Racecar driver Larry Thomas was heading for Daytona to drive in speedway tire tests when his car was involved in a collision,, jumped a guardrail, and went down a 35-foot embankment on Interstate 75 in Tifton, Ga., killing him early on the morning of January 25, 1965. He was 28.

A resident of the Tabernacle area of Randolph County, Thomas had been racing full-time for three years and was a member of The Pure Oil Club at Darlington, S.C., which was limited to outstanding stock car drivers. Many leading race drivers attended his funeral and several served as pallbearers when he was buried at Tabernacle Cemetery on Old Highway 64 (Secondary Road 1344). A picture of a race car decorates his tombstone.

* * *

Buren Skeen was critically injured the first time he drove in one of the most prestigious stockcar races of all, the Southern 500 at Darlington, S.C. That was on Labor Day, 1965. He died six days later, 15 days short of his 29th birthday.

"When the green flag dropped, he roared off in quest of the pot of gold at the end of the rainbow," wrote Publisher Ed Wallace in the *Denton Record* . "Two laps later he found eternity."

A 10-year veteran of Modified Sportsman Racing, Skeen had moved up to the Grand National Circuit the year he died. According to Wallace, "The Denton native started racing in 1954 and his love of racing took him to most of the tracks in the South. He raced once at Daytona, was twice Bowman Gray and State Sportsman Champion, but 1965 was his biggest year."

Skeen is buried at Lineberry Methodist Churchyard at Handy, a small community along N.C. Highway 109 in southern Davidson

155

In Randolph County is the gravestone of
David E. Ridge, an avid fisherman.

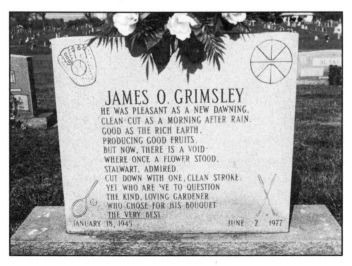

Asheboro lawyer James O. Grimsley, who collapsed
and died while running, enjoyed a variety of sports.

County. A racecar with the number 71 on the door is carved into one side of his granite stone with his name above it.

* * *

Gift shops occasionally sell ornamental plaques bearing this thought: "God does not count against man's alloted time on earth the hours he spends fishing."

Fishing makes its way onto many tombstones, the most common epitaph being:

Gone Fishing.

One person buried under those words is Joe Prevost "Junebug" Swaim of Randleman, who for many years operated a barbershop on Main Street.

"He liked fishing so much, that you knew doggone well that he would close up his shop and go right then if you suggested it, even if he had another customer waiting for a haircut," Charlie Russell of Randleman recalled.

Swaim is buried at Mt. Lebanon Church Cemetery on West River Drive, across Deep River from the location of his tiny shop.

* * *

A scene of a man in a rowboat pulling a fish from a lake with a cane pole decorates the tombstone of R.L. Williams, 1924-1985, at Albemarle Street Cemetery in Edenton in Chowan County.

* * *

An elaborate engraving on the headstone of Carlos Howell at Raleigh's Oakwood Cemetery shows an angler standing in an anchored motorboat pulling in a fish. Howell died on Sept. 9, 1982, when he fell overboard while boating near Atlantic Beach in coastal Cartaret County on a day with strong winds and tides.

* * *

157

Among the most highly admired memorials to fishermen in North Carolina is that of David E. Ridge of Farmer in Randolph County. Ridge, who was 69, died on May 1, 1969, while on the way home from a fishing trip with his fishing buddy, the late H.P. "Hub" Kearns, who lived near him.

"Mr. Ridge was driving," Kearns' wife later recalled. "Hub got out of the car and got his fishing box and a string of fish out of the trunk. I heard him say 'So long' to Mr. Ridge, and then Hub came in the house. We talked about the trip for about ten minutes, then Hub started putting his stuff away. I happened to look out the window and said, 'Hub, I wonder why Mr. Ridge is still parked in the driveway? Do you suppose he has car trouble or something?' Hub went out to see if Mr. Ridge needed help and found him slumped over the steering wheel. Apparently he had had a heart attack and passed away."

Ridge's tombstone at Hoover Grove Cemetery along Secondary Road 1314 east of Jackson Creek depicts a fishing scene, but the epitaph is what makes it memorable:

God grant that I may live to fish
Until my dying day
I then most humbly pray
That in His mercy
I be judged good enough
To keep.

A Few Unique Tar Heels

Christopher Hill figured if he built a fence of rocks, he'd never have to replace it. Hill lived on a ridge west of Little Caraway Creek in Randolph County that offers one of the most picturesque views in the Uwharrie Mountains. Southeast are Mt. Shepherd, Caraway Mountain, and numerous smaller ridges that seem to roll on endlessly.

According to a historical pamphlet compiled in 1977 by Vera Hughes for the Poplar Ridge Alumni Association, Hill "needed some way to keep his goats from roaming too far astray. Having plenty of loose rocks on his farm, he and a small son, Thomas, built a wall."

More than a century and a half later, people still marvel over that wall and it is even noted on Hill's tombstone at Mt. Gilead Methodist Church Cemetery just north of his farm.

CHRISTOPHER HILL. 1804-1856
He Built A Rock Wall
One Mile Long
One Mile South
Of Here.

"A part of the wall...is right here," said Wade Kindley, who now lives on part of what was once Christopher Hill's huge farm, as he led the way past his barn and along a shady lane. "This was the old dirt road section, the old road to High Point. To the left is the high bank where you can still see large rocks laid in a pattern. This is now part of the Dallas Rush property. But the rock fence ran from that big brick house up there, the Ted Hanes place, came back of Tom Osborne's, and then on my property for about 500 or 600 feet before it got to the Rush place. It ran all the way to near Poplar Ridge Church. All of this

159

land, as far as you can see, was Christopher Hill's at one time. It is said he bought the whole place by trading two colt mules and giving $60 to boot for it!"

The road that ran alongside became known as "The Rock Fence Road," and over the years many stories were connected with it. The Poplar Ridge pamphlet mentions that "Blanche Johnson remembers seeing John Briles and Effie Welborn courting in a buggy on Rock Fence Road about 1890....

"...Henry Royals was a familiar figure in his horse-drawn mail buggy coming along Rock Fence Road...

"When Louise Hill and George Rush decided to marry, it did not meet with family approval, so Louise bundled up the wedding clothes, hid them behind a tall boulder adjacent to Rock Fence Road and there dressed for her wedding."

The "Wedding Gown Boulder" is still on Wade Kindley's property, jutting prominently out of the south pasture, a few feet from the old rock fence line.

"But a great deal of the fence rocks are gone," Kindley said. "My wife's father, Commodore Crotts, let the state highway crews take as much as they wanted to crush to use for road paving gravel 50 years ago."

Howard Hoover of Asheboro, a retired highway construction man who worked in the Poplar Ridge area from 1931 to 1938, said, "I don't remember if my road crew of convicts worked on Rock Fence Road or not. But we did use portable rock crushers in those days and got field rocks to crush as we went along."

"What's left of the fence is a line of loose rocks, mostly scattered over the years by hunters," said Kindley, as he stooped to pick up an 18-inch chunk. "I reckon this smaller one might have been one of the stones from Hill's rock wall." He carried it back to his house on Secondary Road 1408, known as Hoover Hill Road, and used it to prop open his yard gate.

* * *

Abigail (Mrs. Horatio H.) Willis, who died October 12, 1864, was the mother of four children, one of whom was killed when nearby Fort

Macon was overrun by federal troops during the Civil War. Before her death, she made arrangements to call attention to herself from the grave.

Her tombstone in The Old Burying Ground at Beaufort in Carteret County hails passersby:

BEHOLD!
IT IS I,
ABIGAIL!

* * *

A newspaperman, philosopher, and author in Southern Pines, Bion H. Butler didn't mind when folks called him a "tramp printer." Born in New York in 1857, he learned to set type at age 12 and had started his own newspaper at 19. A globe trotter, he and his wife settled in Moore County in 1890. As he had done elsewhere, he promptly carved a name for himself in the Tar Heel press, writing for local and state papers. The author of two books, *The Church on Quintuple Mountain* and *Old Bethesda: At the Head Of Rockfish,* he was editor of the Southern Pines *Pilot* at the time of his death in 1935 at 77.

When writer Clyde Davis left Southern Pines for a newspaper job in New York, he wrote in a parting note that he had hoped to live and die in Moore County in the vicinity of Mount Helicon, where after death he, Bion Butler, and another friend, James McNeil Johnson, could sit on their tombstones at Bethesda Cemetery on moonlit nights and enjoy one another's company.

Butler is indeed buried at Bethesda Cemetery east of Aberdeen along N.C. Highway 5, along with Johnson, but Clyde Davis never returned to the Sandhills, not even in death. If Butler and Johnson visit from their tombstones by night, Butler has a comfortable seat, for his stone is a large boulder bearing a plaque that proclaims him:

The Sage of the Sandhills.

* * *

161

Twice Robert Harrell was buried at the same spot in the foothills of Cleveland County, but many thought he deserved to be buried yet a third time—near the ocean that he loved. And 17 years later he was.

A resident of Shelby, Harrell radically changed his life in the mid-1950s at age 63. He changed his name from Harrill to Harrell and took up beachcombing at Fort Fisher. For 16 years he lived a solitary life, becoming widely known to summertime beach crowds as "The Fort Fisher Hermit." Untold thousands of vacationers visited him at his makeshift home in an abandoned, concrete military bunker.

He died there in 1972, eight months shy of his 80th birthday. His death was attributed to natural or unknown causes, and no autopsy was performed. His son, George Edward Harrill, thought, however, that someone may have caused his father's death during a robbery attempt, for it was thought Harrell sometimes stashed away money given to him by tourists.

Harrell's body was taken back to Cleveland County and buried at Sunset Cemetery in Shelby, far from his beloved beach. A marker was put on his grave, correctly spelling his family name but identifying him as "The Fort Fisher Hermit." Another line also was added:

He Made People Think.

George Harrill remained doubtful about the cause of his father's death and managed to get the State Bureau of Investigation to open an inquiry in 1980, but no new evidence was uncovered. In 1984, 12 years after Robert Harrell's death, his son had the body exhumed and sent for an autopsy. The results showed no reason to believe foul play had been involved, and "The "Fort Fisher Hermit" was reburied at Sunset Cemetery.

Four more years passed, and George Harrill never changed his mind that somebody had killed his father. But his hopes "to get the truth out are about zero for that anymore," he said. Harrill also had begun to feel that his father should not have been buried in Shelby. He recalled that his father had once said, "When I die, leave me here at the bunker. Let the crabs get me."

So in the fall of 1988, Harrill made plans to have his father's remains moved back to the beach he had loved so dearly. On June 4,

1989, the 17th anniversary of the day The Fort Fisher Hermit was found dead on the beach, his body was carried back to the coast and buried at Federal Point Cemetery on Dowd Road, west of Kure Beach.

The tombstone accompanied him and now marks the grave, which lies between the ocean and Cape Fear River, where seagulls wing overhead and hurricanes can vent their fury. Many visitors have begun leaving autographed seashells at the grave.

* * *

The next time you get angry enough to throw a rock at a politician, don't. Take the rock to Warren County instead. A former politician there would be happy if you threw the rock in his direction.

Of course, Nat Macon has been dead for more than a century and a half, but he left word that he'd appreciate having a stone tossed on his resting place when visitors came to call. His grave is on Secondary Road 1348 about four miles north of Vaughn along U.S. Highway 158. Considering that folks have been throwing rocks on his grave for such a long time, the pile is getting mighty big. Indeed, it's hard to read Nat Macon's epitaph because his tombstone is almost covered with rocks.

If the curious visitor does take time to uncover the granite marker with its bronze tablet, the name Nathaniel Macon comes into view with the dates 1751-1837. Other parts of the tablet state that he was:

> *A soldier of the Revolution.*
> *State Senator 1782, and Speaker*
> *of the House 1801-1807. United*
> *States Senator 1815-1828 and*
> *President Pro Tem of the Senate*
> *1826-1828. President of the*
> *Constitutional Convention of 1835.*
> *"The strictest of our models*
> *of the genuine Republicanism.*
> *Nathaniel Macon upon whose tomb*
> *will be written: Ultimum Romanorumth*
> *Mas Jefferson."*

163

At right: Friends say that the epitaph for Rebecca Holt, buried in Harnett County, fit her perfectly. Below, the grave of the 'Fort Fisher Hermit,' Robert E. Harrill.

ROBERT E. HARRILL
THE FORT FISHER HERMIT
"HE MADE PEOPLE THINK"
FEB. 2, 1893
JUNE 4, 1972

Above, the grave of Nathaniel Macon in Warren County. At left, the headstone for 'Thankful Ann,' in Guilford County.

Despite his high positions, Nathaniel Macon was a humble man. He could have served as an officer in the Revolutionary War, but he turned down a commission, saying he would rather be a private among ordinary soldiers. He could have lived in a mansion after the war, but he said a plain farmhouse suited him fine. He could have sat on the porch sipping mint juleps and watching slaves work in the fields. Instead, he rolled up his sleeves and went out in the broiling sun to work alongside them.

Macon was born in 1751, when North Carolina was still a colony of England. He fought in the War of Independence and afterwards went home to farm. Educated at Princeton, he sought to serve his neighbors, and they elected him to Congress, where he was the only Tar Heel ever to hold the post of Speaker of the House. He later served in the U. S. Senate, becoming president pro tempore. Altogether, he spent 37 years in Congress. Still active at 84, Macon was chosen to represent the state at the 1835 Constitutional Convention, his final federal post.

At home, Macon's stature was such that many people considered him the greatest man North Carolina ever produced. Macon County was named for him, as was the town of Macon in his home county of Warren. When he died in 1837 at 86, he was buried on the grounds of his farm. His wife Hannah Plummer later was buried alongside him.

Tradition tells that Nat Macon once praised rocks as being as beautiful and worthy as flowers. After his death, he said, he'd as soon that people brought rocks to his grave as flowers. "Don't bring a flower," he said. "Let it live. Bring a rock." Legend has it that that quote was scratched on the first headstone that marked his grave. Whether that was true or not, word got around, and over the years the rocks piled up on Macon's grave and overflowed onto his wife's.

In 1937, a century after Macon's death, Warren County bought the isolated old Macon homeplace. A granite headstone and bronze tablet were erected to dignify the heap of rocks that marked his grave. The tablet makes no mention of Macon's choice of rocks over flowers, but it does bear a quote in Latin, reminding visitors that President Thomas Jefferson once called Macon "The last of the Romans."

* * *

166

Only two words adorn Rebecca Holt's tombstone at Barbeque Church Cemetery in Harnett County:

Just Becky.

Friends say the words fit her perfectly.

"She was a sweet kind of woman," said Edith Swann, an aunt by marriage. "She was an office worker and was a hard-worker at her church, too. What everyone remembers is that she was a very unassuming person and giving of herself. A beautiful person to be around."

Rebecca Holt never "put on airs." She wasn't even "Rebecca," unless it was necessary to put it on official forms. She was "just Becky" to everyone.

When she died on February 3, 1982, at 42, it seemed only natural to her family that her tombstone should present her just as she had presented herself.

* * *

A mossy marble tombstone in the Buffalo Presbyterian Church graveyard just off 16th Street in Greensboro bears this humble name:

THANKFUL ANN.

Was "Thankful" a description, or was Thankful Ann her name? Many women of her time were named Faith, Hope, or Charity. But Thankful? What was her family name?

Somewhere there may be musty records of Thankful Ann, but until they turn up, her tombstone must suffice for what is known about her.

Born March 26, 1820, she died January 28, 1839, at 18, the "Consort of Joab Hiatt." She bore him twins on January 24, 1839. One child died that day. Ann died four days later, and the second child died four days after that. The babies are buried with her, but there is no marker for Joab Hiatt.

Thankful Ann would seem to have had little to be thankful for.

* * *

Betsy Ross is popularly credited with creating Old Glory, the first American flag. Historians say there is little proof of that and doubt that she did it. But a tombstone at Hawfields Presbyterian Church Cemetery on N.C. Highway 119 in Alamance County may add credence to the claim.

Legend has it that George Washington and a flag committee visited Betsy, who was known to have made flags, at her home in Philadelphia in June, 1776. Washington supposedly had a flag design of red and white stripes with blue, six-pointed stars that he wanted her to sew, but Betsy talked him into using stars with five points, because they made a better design. This story is based mainly on the word of Betsy's grandson, William J. Canby. In 1857, he wrote that he had been told about the flag by his grandmother when she was 84, the year she died in 1836. Historians scoff at the story partly because Canby revealed it 21 years after he had heard it and 60 years after his grandmother supposedly made the first Stars and Stripes.

Consider now the tombstone at Hawfields Church. On it is engraved:

Ann Ross
Wife Of
Stephanius White
Born in Wilmington, Del.
Relative Of Betsy Ross
Age 85 Years.

Next to it is the tombstone of her husband, also born in Wilmington, Delaware:

Stephanius White
July 19, 1725
Christened in old
Swedes Church
Died 1823.

There are no birth or death dates on Ann Ross White's stone, but the years of her life can be calculated from those of her husband, who

168

lived to be 98. Assuming that she was five to 10 years younger than her husband, that would have put her birthdate between 1730 and 1735 and her death between 1815 and 1820. Clearly her life coincided with that of Betsy Ross, who lived from 1752 to 1836. At any rate, she would have died well before W. J. Canby said he heard his grandmother tell about the flag episode. Why would Ann Ross White have wanted to tell the world about her relationship with Betsy Ross by way of her tombstone unless she knew that Betsy Ross could claim a proud moment in her country's history?

* * *

A slave who played an integral part in the founding of Mars Hill College in Madison County is buried on the college's campus in the town of Mars Hill. A memorial boulder covers his remains. Carved on the huge rock are these words:

In Memory Of
JOE.
A Slave Who Was Taken
By The Contractors Of
The First Building Of
This College As A Pledge
For The Debt Due Them.
1856.

Joe's story began in the early 1850s when a number of families in the mountains of Western North Carolina decided that they wanted their children in a Baptist school instead of the Methodist-affiliated academy most had been attending. Edward Carter's family was among these. One day Carter mentioned the families' desires to a prominent Baptist visiting the area, and he suggested that the group raise money to build a school by getting subscriptions.

Carter asked friends and neighbors to support the school and pledged $100 himself. The second person to sign up was the Rev. J.W. Anderson, who had a slave named Joe, who would later figure significantly in the deal.

When $2,000 was pledged, an Asheville contractor was hired to

The gravestone for Joe is located on the Mars Hill College campus.

build the school. But when the work was finished, the group turned up $1,200 short. The group tried to come up with a plan to liquidate the debt, but the contractor was in no mood to wait. He went to court to collect, and he knew just what he wanted as security for his debt: Rev. Anderson's slave, Joe.

When the sheriff served the papers, he took a surprised Joe into custody. Such action was called "levying" in those days and was one means of getting payment for unpaid debts. If the debtors couldn't come up with payment within reasonable time, the security—in this case, Joe—would be turned over to the creditors. Joe was kept in the Asheville jail until he could be sold at auction.

But some of the trustees of the school that was eventually to become Mars Hill College dug into their own pockets and paid the debt so that Joe, one of the few slaves in the mountains, could be returned to his owner.

After the Civil War, Joe was given a lifetime right to a small tract along Gabriel's Creek, where he lived for 40 more years, doing odd jobs around the community. The year of his death was not recorded.

His birth date had never been known either. So it was surmised he was born sometime in the 1830s and died in the first decade of the 1900s.

According to the late John Angus McLeod, a long-time faculty member at Mars Hill College and author of *From These Stones,* Joe was buried in an old, overgrown graveyard on the farm of Leonard J. Huff, not far from his home. Some 15 years later, Joe's son, Neilus, led McLeod to the grave, and a record was made of the location. Joe had been buried in a section of the graveyard with unmarked graves, and only Neilus knew which mound was his father's.

In the summer of 1932, 76 years after he had been a human bond for the debt of Mars Hill College, Joe's remains were removed from the Huff Cemetery and reburied on the college campus. C. M. Palmer of Albemarle donated the huge granite slab that became the marker for his new gravesite.

His impressive new tombstone was unveiled on October 12, the annual Founders' Day at Mars Hill, in ceremonies attended by Joe's descendants.

Mysteries
and Misunderstandings

If divers ever come across an old but unused gravestone in the waters of Salmon Creek in coastal Bertie County, the mystery of Tombstone Point may finally be solved.

A navigational landmark for more than 150 years, Tombstone Point lies at the mouth of Salmon Creek in Albermarle Sound. Maps show its existence as early as 1852. Legend has it that the point got its name from an incident that occurred early in the 19th Century.

The first settlers in the flat coastal area had to order tombstones from England because stone was scarce in the sandy area. According to the legend, the grieving widow of a pioneer ordered one for her husband, but in the many months that passed before it arrived by sailing ship, she had remarried and refused to accept or pay for the stone. Angry and not wanting to haul the stone back, the captain of the ship decided to throw it overboard as he left port. He did so as the ship left Salmon Creek and headed into Albemarle Sound. When word got around about the captain's action, the place was ever after called Tombstone Point.

One person who has tried to confirm the legend is Melvin R. Cobb, a local historian and genealogist, who lives along upper Salmon Creek. In a letter to *State* magazine in February, 1987, Cobb wrote: "Tradition has it that the grieving widow of the tale was Celia Leary, neé Raynor. She was the widow of Thomas Leary, who died in 1815. After Mr. Leary's death, Celia married Michael Capeheart."

In an interview a few months later, Cobb said he had heard some of the descendants of those he named in his letter "have strong feelings that such was not the case."

"I did not say I was certain," he said, "just that legend and some preliminary research points to the people I mentioned."

The answer to the mystery may lie in the eelgrass at the bottom of the bay.

* * *

If William Barnes of Gaston County lived as long as claimed on his tombstone in the old section of the graveyard at Olney Presbyterian Church off U.S. 321 in southeastern Gastonia, he must be the oldest American on record. Nothing is known about him other than what is contained in his epitaph:

In Memory
William Barnes
Who Died September the 7, 1823.

Hark from the tomb a doleful sound,
My ears attend the cry.
Living men come view the ground
Where you must shortly lie.

Aged 218 Years.

* * *

Shortly after a tombstone was erected for Ella Letson in Fair Bluff Cemetery, dark stains began to appear on the marble shaft. The stains finally created an outline of a head.

Some people say that late on hazy mornings, when sunlight is muted, they can also see a faint outline of a face. And back when nocturnal visits were allowed at the graveyard, some observers reported that during full moons, when lunar light shone at an certain slant, they too could see the face. Even Ella Letson's family became upset, so marked was the resemblance to their loved one.

Her family tried to wash the stains off with strong solutions of

Some say that dark stains on this tombstone for Ella Letson in Columbus County are in the shape of Letson's head.

caustic soaps, but although they managed to distort the figure slightly and lighten the shadows, the stains soon darkened again.

The silhouette that is supposedly a likeness of Ella Letson's head on her tombstone has piqued curiosity since she died in 1911 at 27, drawing many visitors to her grave along Secondary Road 1360 off U.S. Highway 76 at Fair Bluff in Columbus County.

"Years ago when passenger trains stopped here, many people got off to visit Ella's grave; then they'd catch a later train to continue on their way," recalls Louise Thomason who works at Fair Bluff's library. "I'd guess that fewer people stop at the graveyard nowadays. Those that do are probably making a side trip while driving to or back from the beaches. Once, when people had fewer things to occupy their time, visiting the graveyard to see the face was a diversion. I know I went up there to show the face to many people. And years later my daughter went up there with her friends. I don't remember why they did it, but my daughter said she and her friends used to leave a candle burning on on Ella's grave..."

Fair Bluff being a town of only 1,000 population, the legend of Ella Letson still looms large. Some believe that she was killed by a train approaching from the east as she stood on the railroad tracks facing west and daydreaming of the day her husband would return from a long trip by rail.

Actually she died from illness. And not at Fair Bluff. According to *Recollections And Records*, a volume commissioned in 1980 by officials of Columbus County and edited by Ann Courtney Ward Little, Ella Jenkins Letson died of tuberculosis while living in Henderson County.

The story began in the early 1900s when Ella's brother, Oscar, went to Missouri to buy horses. While there, he contracted what was then called "the consumption." Ella and her sister Aletha were afraid that their brother's contagion would spread to them when he returned, so they prevailed on their parents to house Oscar in a separate building nearby. He died in April, 1908. Ella apparently picked up the disease from her brother despite his isolation.

Not long after Oscar's death, Ella married M. C. Letson, and the couple moved to mountainous Hendersonville in Henderson County. There she soon was stricken with the dreaded ailment and died in

1911. Her body was returned to Fair Bluff and buried at Powell Cemetery, where her brother also was buried.

A year or two after Ella Letson's tombstone was erected, according to *Recollections and Records*, "Dorthey Dick and some local girls discovered that Miss Ella's likeness had appeared on her headstone. They hurried into town to tell the startling news." From then on curious visitors thronged to see the oddity.

"When I was a small girl, there were still people living who knew Ella Jenkins Letson in the flesh," said Louise Thomason. "They said the shape of the head on her tombstone is just about like the shape that Ella's was. They said one small stain near the shoulder is identical to a small curl of hair that Ella had at that spot. Another stain looks exactly like the shape of an earbob Ella had worn."

Some see only a slight resemblance to a head on Mrs. Letson's stone, and many attach no significance whatever to the stains. They call the blackening mere coincidence, pointing out that many tombstones of marble, which ages easily, have irregular stains on them.

But oldtimers in Fair Bluff have an answer to the scoffers. Go to the grave of Ella Letson's horse trading brother, they say. There are stains on his tombstone, too. They look just like an English saddle.

* * *

Peter Ney was a man of mystery. Researchers over two centuries have been trying to find out who he really was.

Little wonder. Consider the epitaph on his his tomb in Rowan County:

> *In Memory Of*
> *PETER STEWART NEY*
> *A Native Of France*
> *And*
> *Soldier Of The French Revolution*
> *Under*
> *Napoleon Bonaparte*
> *Who departed This Life*
> *November 15th, 1846*
> *Age 77 Years.*

Peter Stewart Ney is buried at Third Creek Presbyterian Church Cemetery. A brick mausoleum with windows now covers his grave, but for many years it was an ordinary mound with a marble marker exposed to the weather like others in the graveyard.

The big mystery has always been, "Was Peter Stewart Ney really Marshal Michel Ney of Waterloo fame and the right hand man of French Emperor Napoleon Bonaparte?" The answer has always eluded those who tried to put pieces of the Ney puzzle into place.

History says Marshal Ney was executed before a firing squad in France. But people who knew the Peter Ney of Rowan County believed their neighbor and the Marshal were one and the same.

How could that be?

Late in 1818, Peter Ney appeared in central North Carolina as a school teacher. No one knew where he had lived or worked prior to that time.

Rumor had it that when Marshal Ney of France had been placed before a firing squad, a conspiracy had been hatched for soldiers to shoot over his head and for Ney to feign death by crushing a vial of red liquid under his shirt.

Be that as it may, it is fact that a French ship arriving at Charleston, S.C., on January 16, 1816, had a passenger that was either Marshal Ney or a perfect double. The likeness was affirmed by French citizens who had fled to America earlier and had known the real Ney. Some believe this Ney lived for awhile with a former French military officer in Indiana before coming to North Carolina.

A Ney did settle in Rowan County and taught school between 1819 and 1825. He had all the physical characteristics of Marshal Ney, including red hair. He also knew French history and military strategy. Despite frequent questioning, he always went into silence when asked if he were Marshal Ney. However, he often alluded to being the military officer when under the influence of strong drink. On his deathbed in 1846, he is reported to have told Dr. Matthew Locke: "I am Marshal Ney of France."

Tomb It May Concern

Col. Eziekiel Polk wrote his own epitaph and made sure he mentioned having been "bred" in North Carolina. He also made certain that his caustic observations, written in his 74th year, would be etched in stone. They adorn his grave, at Polk Cemetery in Bolivar, Hardeman County, Tennessee.

Here lies the dust of Old E. P.
One instance of mortality.
Pennsylvania born, CAROLINA BRED.
In Tennessee died on his bed.
His youthful days he spent in pleasure
His later days in gathering treasure.
From superstition liv' d quite free
And practiced strict morality
To hold cheats was never willing
To give one solitary shilling.
He could forsee and in forseeing
He equals most of men in being.
That church and state will join their pow' r
And misery on this country show' r
And Methodists in their camp brawling
Will be the cause of this down falling.
An era not destined to see.
It waits for poor posterity.
First fruits and tithes are odious things
And so are bishops, priests and kings.

E. P. Polk, who died on August 31, 1824, two years after writing his epitaph, was a Tar Heel of note. A signer of the Mecklenburg Declaration of Independence, he was commissioned a lieutenant colonel in the South Carolina militia during the Revolutionary War. He left North Carolina after the war to take advantage of the large parcels of land available in Tennessee. He was the grandfather of James Knox Polk, the North Carolina-born President of The United States.

Although Colonel Polk's home in North Carolina has never been pinpointed, it is thought that he lived in the same area of southern Mecklenburg County where the restored cabin birthplace of his grandson is now a historical site.

* * *

A tombstone has been erected for J. W. "Bill" Johnson of Scotland Neck, and his epitaph is carved upon it. But if he has his way, his tombstone will never mark his grave, because he doesn't want to be buried.

"I would like to be cremated and my ashes scattered around these woods and fields and some thrown into the Roanoke River," said Johnson, a retired forest ranger and wildlife protector, as he stood on the porch of his cabin in Halifax County looking down a steep slope to the river.

Johnson's handsome granite marker at his cabin just off North Carolina Highway 561, two miles east of Pender, is engraved with a wild turkey and a deer. He wrote the epitaph himself, putting together phrases from bits and pieces of things he read over the years, including part of an old Indian prayer. It tells what is in his heart:

The Roanoke Rambler
J. W. Bill Johngon
Sept. 28, 1921

Do not stand by this stone and weep;
I am not dead, I'm only asleep.
When you awake in the morning rush,

179

Do not grieve, but hear the hush.
I feel the gentle winds that blow,
And make clear footprints in the snow.
I see the hawks soaring high,
And watch the duck go sailing by.
I see the sunshine that ripens grain,
And feel the gentle, autumn rain.
I watch the birds in graceful flight,
And see the twinkling stars at night.
I feel the restless Roanoke's flow,
But have gone where the wild geese go.
I leave a ripple at the river's bend,
And a legacy to my kids and kin.
Don't stand at my grave and cry.
I am not there and did not die.

* * *

For more than half a century, Penny Windler of Chapel Hill has saluted the Confederate Flag during ceremonies of the United Daughters of the Confederacy. When she must leave this world she doesn't want anyone to forget her loyalty, either. Her epitaph is to be:

I salute the Confederate Flag
With Affection, Reverence
And
Undying remembrance.

She chose the words, she said, because they "compose the official salute to the Confederate flag, the salute that is used at all Confederate functions." A longtime member of the Julian S. Carr Chapter of the UDC, Mrs. Windler says of the Dixie banner, "It is ignorance and prejudice that won't let us display it in public."

But her devotion to it will be carved in stone.

* * *

Robert F. Dabbs of Randolph County created this sundial-like monument.

Monument To Man
Man Rises
Man Lives
Man Dies.

Robert F. Dabbs wrote those words and had them etched on a bronze plaque that he bolted to a monument he built at his farm at Lineberry, off N.C. Highway 22 in Randolph County. A 30-year veteran of a retail furniture business in Greensboro, Dabbs had a home at suburban Forest Oaks but longed to try real country living. In 1979, he bought 40 acres and the old farmhouse of the late Maggie Hackett. He restored part of the house, built a pond, and in the process lost both his heart and soul to rural living.

The wonders of nature got him to pondering his mortality, and that led to a desire to build what looks like a huge sundial of native boulders and smaller rocks. Upon a large, circular area paved with field stones are several large boulders set upright and off center, one of which bears the plaque. When he dies, Dabbs wants to be cremated and to have his ashes scattered at his monument.

Reward!

Prove yourself a better explorer than the author and reward yourself with the knowledge that you were able to find the following epitaphs which he failed to locate but are alleged to exist in North Carolina:

Willie Hicks Was A Good Boy.
—Reported near Tarboro

Capt. Sam Jones' Leg
Which was amputated July 7, 1804.
—Reported near Edenton

He Fought A Good Fight
But His Razor Was Dull.
—Reported near Salisbury

Poor He lived, Poor he died;
Poor He was buried and nobody cried.
—Reported near New Bern

She Was Almost One Of Us.
—Reported near Edenton.

Write the author at P. 0. Box 204, Franklinville, N.C., 27248, and report your find. Should this book be reprinted, the epitaph, upon confirmation, will be included and credit given to the first person reporting it.

Bibliography,
Additional Reading

ALFORD, Lodwick H. *Alford Family History,* Sea Island, Georgia, February 1986. Revised April 1986, February 1987, and June 1987.

AUSTIN, Sherry Owens. "Where Tony's Ghost Returns For His Harp," *The State,* January 1985.

AUSTIN, Sherry. "A Beauty Spot In Downtown Concord," *The State,* March 1986.

BLEDSOE, Jerry. *Carolina Curiosities*, Eastwoods Press, 1984.

"Epitaphs of the Old Burying Ground," *The State,* August, 1984.

EURE, Linda Jordan. "Two Tombstones," Research Paper, James Iredell House Historic collection, Edenton, 1987.

EVANS, W. McKee. *To Die Game: The Story of the Lowry Band, Indian Guerrillas of the Reconstruction,* Louisiana State University Press, 1971.

GOERCH, Carl. column. *The State,* Feb. 17, 1962; column featuring "Obituary," *The Courier-Tribune,* Asheboro, N. C.

HALL, Alonzo C. *Grave Humor*, McNally of Charlotte, 1961.

HOLMES, E. P. *The Disadvantages Of Being A Preacher's Son*, E. P Holmes, 1950; *Angels In Dream Bring Fortune To Aunt Ellen*, E. P. Holmes, 1959.

JONES, H.G. "The Unique Tomb of William Andrews Jeffreys," *The State*, December 1988.

KING, Henry. "Negro Youth Buried In White Cemetery," *Greensboro Daily News*, January 29, 1961; "Hang Your Head Tom, Hang Your Head And Cry," *The Courier-Tribune*, Asheboro, March 19, 1987; "She Was The Best Peach In The Basket," *The Courier-Tribune*, Asheboro, June 23, 1983; "We're All Beholden To Ann Hiatt," *The Courier-Tribune*, Asheboro, Nov. 24, 1977; "Rock Fence Remnant All That Now Remains," *The Courier-Tribune*, Asheboro, May 1, 1986; "Cemetery Sentiment Is Tombstone Tonic," *The Courier-Tribune*, Asheboro, May 30, 1984; "High-in-sky Performer Jumped To A Conclusion," *The Courier-Tribune*, Asheboro, August 22, 1985; "Unforgettable Elephant Tale Gets Retelling," *The Courier-Tribune*, Asheboro, Nov. 19, 1987; "Marble Marker Monument To Long-Ago Boy Scout," *The Courier-Tribune*, Asheboro, Nov. 7, 1985; "History Lost Their Names To Fickle Finger Of Fate," *The Courier-Tribune*, Asheboro, Jan. 17, 1985; "Between A Rock And A Resting Place," *The Courier-Tribune*, Asheboro, Feb. 12, 1987; "Ramblings In Randolph," *The Courier-Tribune*, October 8, 1968; September 18, 1970; "Not Much Is Known About Him, But One Thing Is Clear," *The Courier-Tribune*, Oct. 2, 1988; "Old Burying Ground Has The Unusual, Bizarre," *The Courier-Tribune*, Asheboro, September 26, 1974; "'Soldier Of France' Mystery Unsolved," *The Courier-Tribune*, Asheboro, August 5, 1982.

LEE, Lawrence. *The History of Brunswick County, N.C.*, reference library, Brunswick Town State Historic Site.

LITTLE, Ann Courtney Ward, editor. *Recollections And Records*, Columbus County Bicentennial Commission, 1980.

McLEOD, John Angus, Sr. *From These Stones,* Mars Hill College,

1955. (Revised/updated 1968.)

MEDLEY, Mary Louise. Untitled article (Wong Bow grave), *The State*, "Anson's Civil War Dr. Beeman." Also, "Civil War Physician Fed His Fever Patients, Unheard Of Practice." *The Messenger and Intelligencer,* Wadesboro, Anson County bicentennial features, 1949.

MOOSE, Debbie. "Tombstone Territory,"*News And Observer,* Raleigh, Nov. 23, 1987.

North Carolina: A Rich Heritage. Literary Works by Young Authors. Vol. II. N.C. Council International Reading Association, 1985.

Old Burying Ground, Beaufort Historical Association, 1965

"Oldest Gravestone," letter, *The State,* Nov. 1, 1967.

PARKER, Cherry. "He Fed Fever," *The State,* September 1987.

PAYSOUR, Conrad, "Guilford Man Found Place In Railroad Lore," *Greensboro Daily News*, Jan. 3, 1984.

"Peaches and Fever," *The State*, March 5, 1960.

PLEASANTS, Paul. "Our Most Famous Residents," *The State*, April 29, 1961.

"Primitive Baptists; Pocahontas; And A High Diver...," *The State,* Feb. 29, 1964.

RAYNOR, George. "Irreverent Polk Composed His Own Epitaph," *Salisbury Post*, March 17, 1985.

ROGERS, Dennis. "A Century Later, The Saga of Mille-Christine Is Still Told," *News and Observer,* Raleigh, Jan. 31, 1984; "Diaries Keep Alive Memories of Siamese Twins," *News And Observer,* Raleigh, March 8, 1984; "Unearthing The Feats Of Life At The Home

Of The Dead," *News and Observer*, Raleigh, March 31, 1981; "Southern Heroine Stole Men's Hearts And Their Secrets," *News and Observer,* Raleigh, Sept 21, 1987; "Harnett Pilot Realized His Dreams, & Others, In Flight," *News and Observer,* Raleigh, Feb. 15, 1988.

SEAY, Majel Ivey. "Murder In The Circus," *The State*, April 1, 1961.

"Slave Helped Found School," *The State,* date unknown.

SNOW, A.C. "In Beaufort They Buried A Brave Young Sailor Standing Up," *News and Observer*, Raleigh, July 16, 1988.

SOUTH, Stanley A. *Colonial Brunswick*, State Department of Archives and History.

SPENCER, Carl. "Odd Facts In Carolina," *Greensboro Daily News*, date unknown; "Tar Heel Stuff," *Salisbury Post*, Nov. 23, 1980, Nov. 5, 1982.

"Tar Heel Information," *The State*, March 1986.

THOMPSON, Herb. "Levi Matthews Was A Railroading Man," *The State,* February 1987.

WILLS, Bob. "From Siamese Twins To Sky Divers," *The State,* Oct. 1, 1968 .